Assimilation Blues

ASSIMILATION BLUES

◆

Black Families
in a White Community

Beverly Daniel Tatum

BASIC
BOOKS

A Member of the Perseus Books Group

A hardcover edition of this book was published in 1987 by Greenwood Press.

Published 1999 by Basic Books, A Member of the Perseus Books Group

LIBRARY OF CONGRESS CATALOG CARD NUMBER 87–241
ISBN 0-465-08360-9

To my sons, Travis Jonathan and David Alexander

Contents

Introduction to the 2000 Edition

I was pregnant with my first child when I began interviewing the families whose lives are at the heart of this book. I came to those interviews not only with the questions of a researcher interested in the socialization of Black children in predominantly White communities but also with the questions of an expectant parent who would soon be faced with a similar challenge herself. Though I had firsthand knowledge of what this experience was like from a child's perspective—after all my family had been one of few Black families in the small New England town where I grew up—I did not have a parent's insight and I was eager for it. My family had "integrated" our previously all-White neighborhood in 1958, but in the 1980's, more than twenty years later, one could still describe my parents and other families like mine as pioneers, pushing the boundaries of societal segregation. Yes, I wanted to know about "socialization strategies" and the maintenance of "extended family relationships" and "fictive kin networks"—topics that Black-family scholars often investigate. But I also wanted to know how to cope with arranging play dates with White parents who may or may not welcome a Black child to their home, what to say to the White teacher who says she is "color-blind" and treats all the children the same ("the same as what?"). I wondered how to talk to a child about name-calling or maybe even interracial dating. I wondered how to foster a sense of pride in one's African-American heritage when there are no visible signs of it reflected in the community. I asked questions as a parent as well as a university researcher, and I learned a lot.

That child is now seventeen, and I can see the many ways my own parenting has been influenced by the experiences shared with me by the mothers and fathers of Sun Beach. I heard their voices as I considered whether to attend the neighborhood (mostly White) church or drive thirty minutes to a predominantly Black congregation in a nearby city. I remembered their words when my son came home from his day-care center, asking "Am I Black?" I thought about their choices and sense of control as I considered whether to send my children to public or private schools. Not all the parents I interviewed would have agreed with my decisions, I'm sure, but I was comforted by knowing that I was not the first Black parent to face these choices. And I made them with the understanding that the choices are meaningful, that they do make a difference to our children.

We live in an era of upward mobility for African-Americans—and in a time of continuing despair. A recent *Newsweek* magazine cover (June 7, 1999) proclaimed "The Good News about Black America (and Why Many Blacks Aren't Celebrating)," highlighting the fact that African-Americans have made significant gains in educational attainment, life expectancy, and family income but still are disadvantaged in comparison to Whites. At the start of the twenty-first century, Black income is at its highest level ever; yet Black unemployment is still twice the rate of Whites, and many Black families struggle below the poverty line. Similarly, polls examining Americans' changing views on race and racial tolerance indicate more positive attitudes of Whites toward Blacks yet the media continues to report news of increasing racial violence. Middle-class Black families living in predominantly White communities often live in the nexus between these two realities. While their own incomes have risen, they often have ties to extended family in less affluent circumstances. And though improving race relations have made their move to formerly all-White communities possible, they still may be subject to varying degrees of hostility and/or exclusion in these communities.

The dilemma is tragically embodied in the life and death of Isaiah Shoels, the young African-American man who was murdered along with other students at Colombine High School in a shooting spree orchestrated by two of their classmates. Isaiah's upwardly mobile family moved to Littleton, Colorado, because of the town's safe and tranquil suburban atmosphere. One of few Black children in his high school, Isaiah was targeted by his teenage assassins because of his race. While such acts of violence can happen anywhere, this incident captures the potential nightmare of isolation even as the move to a community like Littleton represents for some the dream of integration.

Residential segregation remains one of the most persistent manifestations of racism in American society. Though residential segregation has decreased somewhat since the 1970's, most racial and ethnic groups in the United States still live disproportionately with members of their own group. Black families are more likely to live in segregated neighborhoods than other people of color. When they live in predominantly White communities, their experiences can range from the pleasantly benign (as mine has been) to the horrendous. We need to know more about the context of those experiences and how families and children respond to them. Since the original publication of this book in 1987, psychologists, sociologists, and journalists like Nancy Boyd Franklin, Joseph Feagin, and Ellis Cose, to name a few, have explored life among the Black middle class, but often the focus is on those who live in Black suburban enclaves like those in Maryland's Prince George's County or outside major metropolitan areas. *Assimilation Blues* remains one of the few examinations specific to a predominantly White context.

I am delighted *Assimilation Blues* is being reissued, because it means the lessons of the families of Sun Beach will be available to yet another generation of parents (and friends, neighbors, and teachers) of Black families in White communities. Their experiences continue to be important because the questions remain. How do Black families cope with the isolation they often feel in mostly White communities? What advocacy is needed in schools that are sometimes insensitive to what it means to be one of a handful of Black students, perhaps the only Black student in the classroom? What strategies make sense as we begin the twenty-first century? The families that have staked their claim on the edge of integration have stories to tell and lessons to teach that need to be heard by all of us.

Acknowledgments

An obvious debt of gratitude is owed to the families who so generously made the time to talk with me, and whose openness and honesty made this book possible. Much of what they had to share has not only enriched these pages, but has helped to broaden my perspective on my own life experiences in a predominantly White community.

The work of two scholars, Harriette Pipes McAdoo and Wade Nobles, deserves special acknowledgement. Their inquiries into the lives of Black families served as models for my own.

A number of people read the manuscript at various stages of its preparation. My thanks to all for their useful suggestions and words of encouragement, especially Eric Bermann, Walter Allen, Philip Bowman, and Mary Whiteside. I also want to thank Elise Magnuson and Deborah Ross for their assistance with the preparation of this manuscript.

I must acknowledge the tremendous love and support I have received from my family. My parents, Robert and Catherine Daniel, have always been there when I needed child care assistance (or anything else!). My brothers and sister offered encouragement and assistance along the way. But without a doubt, this book would never have been completed without the help of my husband, Travis James Tatum, whose excellent parenting of our children gave me the space to work, whose willingness to read and re-read the text gave me the distance to edit, and whose hugs gave me more energy when I really needed it.

Above all, I want to thank the Spirit that spoke to me in the night, and made this book possible.

1

Invisible Families and Black Family Research

What does it mean to be a middle-class Black parent living, working and raising children in the midst of a predominantly White Community? Does it mean opportunity, success, the "American Dream" realized, or is it rootlessness, isolation, and alienation? Is it some combination of all these things? These questions hit at the core of the experiences of upwardly mobile Black families, yet to ask such questions is to make a significant departure from traditional Black family research. Although what has often been erroneously referred to as "the Black family" has been the subject of scientific inquiry since before the turn of the century, the Black family that has been most often investigated has been the poor Black welfare family that lives in a urban ghetto or, on occasion, the poor Black family that lives in the rural South. There is no one Black family, yet families whose life patterns have varied from those just described have been "invisible" to family researchers and social scientists who have largely overlooked their lives and experiences.

The omission of these invisible families in the field of Black family study stems from the social and political context in which the research has been done. Historically, Black families have been treated as a social problem for which a solution must be found (Billingsley, 1973). The view that Black families are different from White families in very negative and potentially destructive ways, a view that has been labelled the "cultural deviant" perspective (Allen, 1979), dominated the literature, resulting in the research emphasis on the "problem" Black family.

Other perspectives, such as the "cultural equivalent" and the "cultural variant" approaches, have also been represented in the literature. The former approach assumes that Black families are essentially the same as White families, with the effects of social class accounting for any apparent differences. The latter approach assumes that Black family life *is* culturally distinctive due to its particular historical and sociocultural context, but does not assume those distinctions to be necessarily pathological (Allen, 1979). The cultural variant perspective has been used increasingly in the more recent Black family research. While both of these perspectives are conceptually less problem-oriented, even those who incorporated them into their research still tended to focus on the same kinds of families that were the subjects of the deviance-seekers.

While unquestionably both the urban and rural poor constitute a significant portion of the Black population, their over-representation in the literature, concurrent with the relative neglect of other kinds of Black families, has led to a distorted view of Black families in America. There have, however, been important exceptions in this trend which should be noted. Researchers such as McAdoo (1978), Landry and Jendrek (1978), Cazenave (1978), and Willie (1981) have explored aspects of family life among upwardly mobile or middle-class Blacks. The value of such research should be obvious. "Generic" family researchers have long since abandoned the idea of a single, normative or model American family, yet some social scientists have been slow to recognize that there are "as many different familial forms among Afro-Americans as there are different Afro-American ex-periential and phenomenal realities" (Myers, 1982, p.36). Since no one segment can represent the whole, our understanding of families in general, and Black families in particular, requires that this diversity be acknowledged.

However, even the research on middle-class Black families has generally been done with sample populations that were embedded in larger Black communities. Although a case study of a Black family in a predominantly White community is included in Willie's *A New Look at Black Families* (1976) and articles about such families have appeared in newspapers and magazines (Williams, 1985; "Roots III," 1985), there has been little previous examination of the existential and phenomenal realities of those Black families living outside the context of a larger Black community.

Exactly how many Black families could be characterized in this way is unknown. Though over 6 million of the nation's 26.5 million Blacks live in suburban areas, and the numbers are increasing, the majority of them are located in racially mixed suburban communities near central city areas (Williams, 1985). Patterns of residential segregation within those areas may still create Black communities, but as a Black person who has lived in three different communities, all of which have negligible Black populations, and having talked with others with similar experiences, I believe that there are many Black families among that group of suburbanites that live and work in relative isolation from other Blacks, and that the number is increasing.

Why they come, where they come from, and how they perceive themselves in relation to each other and the rest of their environment are but a few of the broad questions that need to be asked and placed in the context of family life. What *does* it mean to be a middle-class Black parent living, working, and raising children in the midst of a predominantly White community? An effort to answer this question will help to add an important missing piece to the larger picture of Black families in America.

The research presented in the following chapters is intended as a first step in this process. Because of the lack of existing literature about this particular segment of the Black population, the study on which this book is based was designed to be exploratory in nature, generating hypotheses rather than testing them. It is a study, conducted in 1981, of 10 invisible Black families living in a California community I have called Sun Beach, a fictitious name for a very real community of 70,000 people, in which only 2.4 percent of the population is Black.

Certainly a study of 10 families in one community can not and should not provide all the answers to the questions asked in the opening of this chapter. Premature generalizations from limited data have too often been the hallmark of Black family research. However, an in-depth examination of the lives and experiences of these husbands, wives, and their children can and should help clarify and refine the questions that need to be asked. The responses that both parents and children provided in the lengthy interviews which formed the core of this study clearly raise issues that reach far beyond the Sun Beach city limits, and have immediate relevance for Black families, regardless of where they live.

While there is no question that the experiences of middle-class Blacks in the midst of White America have been neglected in social science literature, there has been research that highlights issues one might anticipate would be relevant to a discussion of those experiences. This research can be divided into the following three topic areas: 1) the extended family and the Black middle class, 2) social stresses and Black families, and 3) biculturation and the Black community as a socializing agent. Each of these areas will be discussed.

THE EXTENDED FAMILY AND THE BLACK
MIDDLE CLASS

A recurrent theme in many studies of Black families, regardless of the theoretical perspective used, has been the importance of extended family relationships (Myers, 1982). Martin and Martin (1978) defined a Black extended family as

> a multigenerational, interdependent kinship system which is welded together by a sense of obligation to relatives; is organized around a "family base" household; is generally guided by a "dominant family figure"; extends across geographical boundaries to connect family units to an extended family network; and has a built-in mutual aid system for the welfare of its members and the maintenance of the family as a whole. (p.1)

Although certainly strong extended family ties are found among other ethnic groups, this particular feature of Black families is the one most often recognized by researchers as a major characteristic in the differentiation of Afro-American and Euro-American families. The fact that Blacks had more frequent contacts with a greater number of relatives, were more likely to have relatives (particularly siblings or the children of siblings) living with them, and received more child care assistance from relatives than a comparable sample of Whites was demonstrated by Hays and Mindel (1973). A number of anthropological studies have supported this finding (Aschenbrenner, 1975; Hannerz, 1975; Shimkin, Louie, and Frate, 1978; Stack, 1974).

Although there seems to be general agreement that such a pattern exists, why it exists continues to be a debatable subject. Are these extended family support systems a resourceful adaptation to the forces of social exclusion and poverty as Billingsley (1968), Stack (1974), and others have suggested or do they represent a cultural pattern that has its roots in the kinship systems and collectivistic culture of West Africa? Wade Nobles (1974, 1978) has worked to provide empirical support for the latter perspective. Gutman's (1976) examination of primary source historical data and the anthropological work represented in Shimkin, Shimkin, and Frate's *The Extended Family in Black Societies* (1978) make a strong case for the possibility of such cultural continuity.

But, even if the character of Black family kinship systems can be conclusively linked to African family forms, the particular oppressive social and economic circumstances that have affected American Black families continue to be a reality. These environmental factors may have provided the motivation to hold on to the supportive kin network, despite mainstream trends in another direction. Consequently, the two perspectives need not be mutually exclusive.

However, another issue related to the question of "adaptation" versus "Africanity" has emerged, and further fuels the debate. Some writers (Stack, 1974; Martin and Martin, 1978) have suggested that the mutual aid networks which are adaptive in the face of poverty can become a liability for the upwardly mobile. When the immediate needs of the extended family conflict with the long-range goals of individual members, a choice has to be made. As an individual struggles to move up, her family may be weighing her down. If family support systems are valued only as an adaptive response to adverse circumstances, then as their circumstances improve, one would expect Black families to make other adaptations and kinship bonds would probably weaken. On the other hand, if these bonds are a valued humanistic expression of African-American culture, one would expect that strong kinship ties would be a phenomenon that could transcend socioeconomic categories. Are extended family ties (whatever their cultural origin) a permanent part of Black family life or are they being cast aside as more Blacks achieve middle-class standards of success?

In the first empirical study of the Black middle class since the days of Frazier's *Black Bourgeoisie* (1957), the work of Harriette Pipes McAdoo (1977) represents an attempt to answer this question. She studied 178 Black middle-class families in both Washington, D.C. and the suburban "new town" households of Columbia, Maryland. Of those, 72 percent were two-parent households and 28 percent were one-parent households. Regardless of the present family structure, the predominant pattern among the families of origin, most of which had been working-class, was the two-parent nuclear household followed by the two-parent extended household. In sharp contrast to Frazier's (1957) description of the "Black bourgeoisie" as a group that had broken with its cultural past, and floundered without an identity to call its own, McAdoo reported that, regardless of location, the Black middle-class families she studied had indeed held onto an important part of their cultural roots. The network of family and kin who had helped them achieve their level of success had not been forgotten.

Not unlike their low-income counterparts, these men and women kept in close touch with their parents, brothers, sisters, and other relatives. They gave and received significant amounts of help in terms of money, child care, and emotional support (McAdoo, 1979). Aschenbrenner (1975, 1978) also found extended families among middle-income groups in Chicago and in southern Illinois with essentially the same organization as that which she had observed among lower-income Black families.

These studies suggest that Black families do indeed value and hold on to extended kinship ties as they become upwardly mobile. McAdoo (1978) goes further to illustrate that the extended family pattern found among the recent middle class, does persist after economic stability has been established for more than one generation. There is no difference in the amount or kind of help received by those families whose origins were working-class and those whose families had been part of the "old" Black middle class.

Of course, the argument could be made that the extended family network among middle-class Blacks is still just an adaptation to particular social stresses. Although their economic circumstances have improved, they still have not achieved financial parity with middle-income Whites. In 1976, the median incomes of Black and White husbands were $11,616 and $17,791 respectively. When Black wives worked full time, their median family incomes increased to $20,916 (Glick, 1981). The fact that Black husbands and wives jointly earn a median income which is only $3,125 more than what a White husband earns alone attests to the greater effort required of Black families to maintain their middle-income status. That Black women are more likely than White women to work outside the home comes as no surprise in the face of such statistics. The unequal rates of pay evidenced in these figures are underscored further by the fact that, while Blacks place a high value on education as an avenue for upward mobility, the income return received by Black males for each additional year of education is only about half that of White males, $333 to $686 (Landry, 1980).

In addition to having lower incomes, Landry (1980) points out that, on the average, the Black middle class has far less accumulated wealth, such as stocks and bonds and reserves in savings, yet has larger debts than the White middle class. The combination of lower incomes, assets and savings, and higher debts creates a situation of economic tenuousness. Scanzoni (1971) suggests that Black families at this socioeconomic level experience a painful sense of "relative deprivation" and alienation as a result of economic discrimination. The family network ties among the middle class may then be held on to because of the still-needed emotional (and perhaps financial) support they give. Viewing community social agencies as not very sensitive or helpful, these families "may work to maintain the shared kin-help network because they sense it will be their only sure source of help in times of future trouble—a kind of 'kin insurance' " (McAdoo, 1979, p. 110).

Just as was the case with the low-income family, the recognition of the extended family's continued usefulness for middle-income Blacks does not preclude the possibility of an African cultural heritage influencing its maintenance as well. At the very least, this and other evidence (Anderson and Allen, 1982) would suggest that the extended family networks are more than just essential coping strategies for those in poverty.

It is interesting to note that most of the family members included in McAdoo's study lived within 30 miles of their parents. Some reported having turned down job promotions in order to stay in the area. This finding might lend support to those who claim that extended family ties can limit economic advancement.

However, in Shimkin, Louie, and Frate's study (1978), they found that the extended family network could also serve as a facilitating agent in migration and urbanization, as well as fostering educational and economic advancement. Another study (Mueller and Ladd, 1970) of Black and White differences in geographic mobility drew a similar conclusion. When Blacks relocate, they are more likely than Whites to move where family and friends have already settled. The family is often the main source of information about employment and educational opportunities. So, while only one-third of the Blacks surveyed lived in the same county in which they were born, 59 percent were living near all or most of their relatives. Only 6 percent (compared to 21 percent) had *no* relatives living in the vicinity (Mueller and Ladd, 1970).

What is the significance of these findings for Black families living in predominantly White communities? Do they represent the apparently small portion of Black families that are without relatives in their vicinity? Are they family trailblazers settling in new areas, eventually to be joined by extended family and friends? Or, unlike the families McAdoo (1977, 1979) described, are these families (for whatever reason) choosing to distance themselves, physically at least, from their kinship networks? If so, what would be the consequences of such a choice?

Does the physical distance between family members lead to breakdown in extended family communication, even when the upwardly mobile family members want to remain emotionally close? In their study of Black extended families, Martin and Martin (1978) described the dilemma of one middle-class couple who found that their friendships, interests, and life style had changed so much that their ties to their families of origin were being sorely strained. Such strains were exacerbated because of the geographical distance between them, making face-to-face encounters few and far between. Family members may interpret such infrequent visits as a purposeful attempt on the part of the upwardly mobile relatives to leave the family behind. Feeling a change in attitude toward them, middle-class members may feel emotionally abandoned by their families "causing a cycle of misapprehension, even if both sides really desire a closer relationship" (p.77). On the other hand, the authors point out that some family members will always consider a relative a part of the family, no matter how far the person has "strayed."

Still, one wonders how intimately connected family members can remain across large geographical distances. Some family isolation may occur, but it would not necessarily have to be total. While there are those who maintain that mobility requires disengaging oneself from the resource-draining process of dealing with the daily needs of one's family, they also acknowledge that such separation does not exclude visiting, joint family celebrations, support of elderly parents or occasional help (McAdoo, 1978).

Assuming a range of patterns of emotional connectedness exists among Black families in predominantly White communities, what accounts for those families who are able to maintain a strong connection to their family base? What adaptation do those families make who cannot? These questions remain, for the moment, unanswered. However, an examination of the family stress and coping literature may shed further light on these issues.

SOCIAL STRESS AND THE BLACK FAMILY

A, a stressor (any unexpected event or situation) combines with B, the family's resources, and C, the family definition of the event, to produce X, the crisis. So theorized Reuben Hill (1963) in his now classic article on social stress and the family. Hill's ABCX family crisis formula is still used as the foundation for research and theory building in this area of family studies (McCubbin, et al., 1980). Despite the continuing use of this formula, it has also been critiqued as inadequate to explain the impact of social stress on some families.

In particular, Peters and Massey (1983) point out the failure of the model to account for the stress of daily survival experienced by those families who must live within a distinctly oppressive environment. The experience of refugee families is used as one case in point. The experience of Black families in America is used as another.

Using Pierce's (1975) concept of a mundane, extreme environment, one in which the many forms of racism and oppression are an ever-present part of daily living rather than occasional hazards (Peters and Massey, 1983), the authors point to discrimination in the areas of education and employment as a major source of what Pierce labeled "Mundane Extreme Environmental Stress" (MEES). Discussing employment statistics like those mentioned earlier in this chapter, they point to the apparent job ceiling that exists for Blacks, frustrating their desires for mobility. Likewise, the educational system, in which so many Blacks put their trust, often betrays them. Rather than preparing their children to compete successfully in the job market, the schools have functioned to track many Black students into educational dead ends.

Using the example of a hurricane, the authors effectively illustrate the need to include the factor of MEES when considering the impact of other sources of stress on Black families. When a hurricane or other natural disaster strikes, it does so without regard for race. Yet one's ability to recover from the disaster may well be influenced by racial determinants. How easily will a Black family find another place to live if their home is demolished? Will emergency assistance be distributed equitably? Will the family be referred by the housing counselor to an undesirable ghetto neighborhood? Will they encounter hostility if they move to an integrated or White area? The subtle (and sometimes not-so-subtle) influence race may have on the family's recovery potential must be considered in any analysis of stressful events in the lives of Black families. Certainly the families in Harriette McAdoo's study (1982) would agree. The respondents in her sample indicated their belief that they experienced extra stress because they were Black.

Perhaps for Black and other oppressed families, a new formula is in order. In fact, Peters and Massey (1983) have used the concept of MEES to expand Hill's ABCX theory. Their new version includes A, the event; A', chronic, unpredictable acts of racism; B, the crisis-meeting resources; C, the family's subjective definition of the event; D, MEES which is anticipated, ongoing and pervasive; all of which combine to produce X, the crisis and Y, the reaction.

Y, the reaction, represents the coping strategies Black families experiencing MEES use to meet the stress/crisis event. Certainly Black families, "perennial refugees" in American society, vary in their vulnerability to racist conditions and environmental stress. Each family develops its own internal coping strategies for dealing with racial oppression. Those strategies that have been effective in the past are passed on to the next generation through the family socialization process. One common coping strategy can be seen in Black parents' attempts to protect their children from racial stereotypes, those negative images reflected by the larger society that can be so damaging to a child's self-esteem. Allies in this effort are the extended family members. Reliance upon them for this and other support is another common coping strategy (Peters, 1976/1977).

Although Black support systems tend to be focused on the family, they can also include co-workers and friends. For women with strong labor force histories, a category which certainly includes Black women, co-worker friends, both male and female, are important potential sources of support (Malson, 1982). Some non-kin relationships become so close that they fulfill family-type functions. Friends become fictive kin, honored with titles such as "play mother" (or father, sister, brother, etc.) to indicate the closeness of the relationship.

The development of fictive kin relationships as a coping strategy is of particular relevance to the issue of Black families who may be geographically and/or emotionally distant from their kinship systems. Co-worker friends and fictive kin represent the evolution of possible alternatives to the extended family support system for those who might need them. Speaking specifically of Blacks who live and work primarily among Whites, however, one might ask how easily they are able to form relationships, supportive enough to have crisis-meeting potential, with their White co-workers and neighbors.

Trust is a critical factor in any close relationship, but it is particularly important for the maintenance of a family-like support system. There are no specific rules governing how the support shall be exchanged. Those "participating often do not know whether they will receive the same services they give, whether the services will be of the same quality, or when in the future they might be called on again to perform a favor" (Malson, 1982, p. 44). Such trust takes time and sustained periods of interaction to develop. Under conditions of MEES, how easily is that kind of trust developed between Blacks and Whites? Would Black families even seek out such close relationships with non-Blacks? If they did, would Whites, perhaps operating with a different cultural framework, be appropriately (from the Black viewpoint) responsive?

The issue of shared (or unshared) frameworks is one considered by Reiss and Oliveri (1983) and forms the basis of their critique of the traditional use of the Hill ABCX formula. Like Peters and Massey (1983), Reiss and Oliveri raise some points which are particularly useful in the consideration of Black families' experiences in a community with a negligible Black population, and may suggest additional coping strategies which become the Y in Peters and Massey's equation.

Family Stress as Community Framework

Acknowledging that family stress is a concept which is difficult to define, Reiss and Oliveri (1983) criticize most family stress researchers for underestimating the impact of the family's own perception of a stressor as a determinant of the degree of stress experienced. How a family defines an event—as an annoying hindrance, an upsetting problem, or a devastating catastrophe—is itself part of the coping process. While one family's problem is another's catastrophe, families who can define a major event as manageable are *already* engaged in an effective coping process. Reiss and Oliveri argue for the need to develop a concept of family stress that is independent of the family definitional process.

The failure to develop such an independent concept of family stress inhibits systematic exploration of what the authors refer to as "generic stress." This term refers to those events which an average family in a particular social community would find stressful. An example of such an event is the closing of a local factory. That some families would cope with the stress of unemployment better than others is, no doubt, true, and examining the perceptions of those more stress-resistant families might help us to understand why. But, the authors point out, it would not help us to understand why this factory closing was disruptive to family life when a similar plant closing in another community was not.

In an effort to remedy this problem, Reiss and Oliveri advocate a community-based approach to defining family stress. Based on the hypothesis that some consensus develops within communities about events taking place within them and their potential effect on families, the authors argue that family stress can be understood, not in terms of the family itself, but in terms of the social community in which the family is embedded. Community, defined as the social settings of the family's everyday life, includes neighborhood, major friendships and kin networks, as well as school and work settings. A consensus about what is and is not stressful develops within the community and provides a shared matrix, a framework for interpreting the seriousness of events.

Given the existence of such frameworks, which may differ from community to community, serious questions are raised about the appropriateness of the construction and research use of stress inventories. When judges are used to measure the "objective" stress inherent in a particular event, in effect what the judges are being asked is, "In *your community*, how much readjustment would these events require?"

An example of the impact of community frameworks can be seen in the assessment of stressful events by Japanese and American judges. In Japanese culture, the honor of one's family is of central importance. A family's honor can be easily tarnished by the actions of one family member. Consequently, minor infractions of the law and a night spent in jail were considered to be much more stressful by the Japanese than by the American respondents. In Japan, such misbehavior affects not only the individual but his family, and results in a more intense experience of shame and loss of status in the community than is the case in the United States (Reiss and Oliveri, 1983).

Recognizing, then, the impact of cultural perspective and community frameworks, it is interesting to consider another possible example. Living under the influence of MEES, would what a Black family experiences as stress in a predominantly White community be considered or understood as stressful by White neighbors, co-workers, or friends? The community, often seen as a resource in Hill's ABCX equation, is not only a potential source of strength and support. It can also be a potential cause of family stress and crisis (Klein, 1983). One would expect the latter possibility to increase in significance when the family does not share the community framework. What might a family's response be to this kind of situation?

Hill (1963) himself wrote that if stress is viewed as being outside the family (as in the case of religious or political persecution), it can solidify rather than disorganize the family. The family may protect itself by withdrawing into itself, maintaining only distant and impersonal neighborhood relationships. Although MEES-experiencing Black families outside the context of a Black community may not necessarily view their environment as a persecuting one, they may see it as an uncertain, potentially hostile one. Consequently, a similar coping strategy—the tightening of family boundaries—might emerge.

Can the family's own style of coping itself become a source of stress? McCubbin and his associates (1980) think so. They identify three ways in which coping could be an additional source of stress. The first method, indirect damage to the family system, could occur if a family member made some bad decisions about the use of family resources, the family savings, for example. The consequence of those decisions would place the family in a disadvantaged, more vulnerable position. Coping methods which lead directly to the breakup of the family would fit in the second category, direct damage to the family system. The third way that coping itself can become a source of stress is if the coping behavior inhibits the development of other adaptive behaviors that would also be helpful to the family.

If, in fact, tightening of Black family boundaries in predominantly White communities takes place, would this pattern of coping be a strength or an additional source of stress? If, as Reiss and Oliveri (1983) suggest, it is adaptive for upwardly (or geographically) mobile families to take as their own the new community's frame of reference, then tightened family boundaries might be an example of the interference to which McCubbin and his colleagues referred. Tightened boundaries would hinder the adoption of a new frame.

But what if the primary frame of the new community is not acceptable? What if the White community frame denigrates or simply does not validate the experiences of a Black family in that setting? Is it adaptive to adopt such a frame or erect barriers against it? Is acceptance or rejection of community frames determined at the level of the family or at the level of the individual? Will Black children who are continually exposed to the community frame in the school system have the same perception of it as their parents do?

What is the impact on the family when parents and children have unshared viewpoints? Hill (1963) provides an example of conflicting parent-child perceptions in his description of desegregation in the South. Both Black and White parents shared a common framework about the nature of appropriate interracial contact which was not always accepted by their children. He writes, "The full blown dimensions of a family crisis are experienced until a new set of norms accepted by both generations develops" (Hill, 1963, p.307).

Learning the family framework (whether the same as the larger community framework or not) is certainly part of the family socialization process. Parents daily provide their children with a set of explanations of the world. Those explanations become critical factors in how children come to understand their own internal and external experiences (Reiss, 1981). Even if children are exposed to alternate or even competing explanations outside of the family, it would seem that this exposure would be mediated by the family's interpretation of the world.

If, however, the explanations or frameworks were, in fact, competing, would the mitigating effect of the family's influence alone be enough to prevent a child's confusion? A discussion of biculturality seems useful here. Defining biculturality as "the ability to function in two worlds," Pinderhughes (1982, p. 114) writes that some Black families are able to function this way quite well. While it requires a lot of effort, families who are comfortable with biculturality "exhibit remarkable flexibility, tolerance for ambiguity, comfort with difference, and creativity in their relationship with both the American mainstream and victim systems." For others, however, the need to function in two worlds leads only to identity confusion and value conflicts.

The process of biculturation, when successful, would seem to allow families and individuals to learn and use, when appropriate, the primary framework of the new community without necessarily abandoning previously learned frameworks. Yet such biculturality may be more easily described than achieved. The factors involved in its development need to be considered further.

BICULTURALITY AND THE BLACK COMMUNITY AS SOCIALIZER

What has just been labelled as "biculturality" has been described by many others since at least the turn of the century, some of whom have preferred terms such as "double-consciousness," "double vision," and "dual reference group orientation" (Cross, 1979). Researchers interested in Black families have discussed the need these families have to consciously (or unconsciously) inculcate such duality in their children (Hale, 1980; McAdoo, 1977; Nobles, 1976). Understanding of exactly how that kind of socialization process takes place is limited, although some work is beginning to be done in that area (Young, 1970; Peters, 1981; Spencer, 1982; Bowles, 1983/1984).

Black parents have to guide their children through conflicting developmental tasks during which the child must internalize the dominant views of our society and at the same time learn to recognize and reach his own potentialities. These tasks are conflicting because the inherent racism of those societal views the children are struggling to internalize is intended to prevent them from reaching the limits of their potential. The inherent difficulty for parents engaged in this socialization process should be apparent. Yet substantial evidence exists that Black families have traditionally been successful in fostering positive feelings of self-worth which are the foundation for self-actualization.

Although the idea that Black children suffer from low levels of self-esteem due to the internalization of the negative images of Blacks fostered by White society is still a popular one, recent reviews of the Black self-esteem and racial identity literature reveal the fallacy of such a notion (Cross, 1978; Porter and Washington, 1979; Jackson, McCullough and Gurin, 1981).

Many of the studies intended to examine the self-esteem and/or racial identification of young Black children used racial preference measures like the Clark's Doll Test, in which children are asked to choose dolls of varying skin colors in response to particular questions. The degree to which the child expressed or did not express preference for the doll with skin color similar to her own was often taken as a direct measure of self-esteem. It appears that this practice represents a major methodological error. Studies in which reference group orientation (racial preference) and self-esteem have been measured independently show that the two have not consistently been related. For example, Black children who clearly showed "light skin color" preference, nevertheless, had self-esteem as high as White children (Cross, 1978). The evidence suggests that group identity and personal identity are two separate issues (Jackson et al., 1981).

Assuming personal identity (who am I) develops before group identity (who are we; who are they) does, the former is more heavily influenced by the character of family relationships. It is the reflected appraisals of intimates within the family circle that lay the groundwork for one's personal identity, to be built on later by peer and other relationships within the community. To the extent that these relationships are with other Blacks, self-esteem can be derived with other Blacks as the primary reference point. Group identity by definition requires a wider reference point. Such a reference point inevitably includes observations of Blacks in interaction with Whites, but the family and immediate community remain important as interpreters of those observations (Jackson et al., 1981).

The importance of the community for the development of positive self/group identity is emphasized by Barnes (1980). Viewing the Black child as embedded in the social system of the Black family, the Black family embedded in the social system of the Black community, and the Black community embedded in the larger White society, Barnes suggests that the Black community forms a protective buffer zone for the family, and consequently the child. This is especially true if both the family and the community share a sense of peoplehood or collective pride.

Black community institutions, particularly religious institutions, serve to reinforce the role of the family in personal identity development. For those families involved, the church provides opportunities for cultural expression and individual growth and development unmatched by other settings, all of which fosters a sense of self-worth and accomplishment for both children and adults (Jackson, 1982).

With these factors in operation, a Black community can develop its own community frame which then reinforces the interpretive frameworks of those families who choose to share in it. In this way, a racially homogeneous environment seems to have positive effects on the self-esteem of Black children. But what about those Black children who are not in a racially homogenous environment? The emphasis that has been placed on the important role of Black communities in personal and/or group identity development certainly raises question about the particular case of Black families living where there is no visible Black community. With the buffer of the Black community removed, is the family's esteem-enhancing capability reduced?

Certainly the family's protective function is tested as the child enters a more heterogeneous environment. The family's ability to filter input from the dominant society is reduced as the child's field of experience broadens. Nevertheless, as the child's contacts with non-Blacks grow in number, the family's role in interpreting those experiences increases. Jackson et al. (1981, p. 259) describe this interpretive role as "critical for maintaining the integrity of the already developed early personal identity as well as the developing conceptions of group identity."

Implicit in this statement is the assumption that the child's earliest development has taken place in the context of a Black reference group. However, this may not be the case for some Black children. In dual career families, children not in the care of extended family members may begin their intergroup contacts very early. Similarly, busy parents without the back-up of the community, and possibly extended family, may not be as effective in interpreting these experiences as they might be in another setting.

If so, what is the impact on the child's personal and/or group identity? It would seem that personal identity, largely shaped by family relationships, could remain intact, and high self-esteem could be maintained. Even if the family is unable to protect the child from negative messages, the psychological distinction between group and personal identity could allow the child to disassociate him/herself from the disparaged group, without sacrificing personal esteem. It is certainly possible that a child could view Black people as generally less worthy than Whites without feeling that she or her family members are inferior. Children learn early that there are exceptions to every rule. "While other minority members may be seen as deserving of societal prejudice, one may view oneself as an exception" (Simmons, 1978, p.55).

What is the psychological consequence of claiming this "exception" status for oneself? As Jackson et al. (1981) point out, no clear relationship between having a strong group identity and psychological well-being has been established. But one might speculate that varying degrees of dissociation may have an impact on the coping mechanisms one uses as an adult. For example, viewing oneself as an exception may be an adaptation that fits the frame of the surrounding White community. To the extent that a Black family conforms to the norms of such a community and does not fit the deviant racial stereotypes that exist in the popular culture, the community may also view the family as exceptional. The phrase, "But you're not like *them*," may have a familiar ring to those in this situation. If the family agrees explicitly or implicitly, "Yes, we're not like *them*," such agreement results in compatible community and family frames. However, when a child socialized with such a framework enters other social arenas, the definition of self as exception may be challenged by those unaware or uninterested in the child's conforming background. What happens then? Does the Black exception have the resources or relevant experience to deal effectively with such challenges?

It is certainly possible that if a child did not experience racism or discrimination and lived in a nonsegregated environment, her sense of belonging to a minority group might be minimized. To the degree that individuality is recognized and appreciated, membership in *any* particular group would become less relevant. In the case of Black children in predominantly White communities, the intergroup environment might actually be relatively nonhostile and nondiscriminatory, particularly if the child is recognized as an exception by the surrounding White community. Parents might be reluctant to raise issues of racism and oppression "unnecessarily" in their effort to shield their children from its effects. Ironically, such efforts may weaken the child's group identity development which may very well be needed as psychological protection in adulthood.

Peters (1981, p.20) wrote that "children must be accepted in the Black community in order to have friends, and they must be accepted in the White community in order to survive." This statement succinctly captures the need Black children have to be bicultural. Do Black parents living in White communities recognize this need? If so, what do they do to see that this need is met? It is clear that there are many issues embedded in this area of research, some of which are beyond the scope of this discussion, but certainly the ones highlighted here further underscore the need for attention to the unique dilemma of Black families living in predominantly White communities.

ORIENTATION TO THE RESEARCH

Given the absence of existing information about Black families in predominantly White communities, the research presented here was not intended to test any particular hypotheses. Instead, my research purpose was to generate data from which critical issues would emerge and from which hypotheses for future research could be more clearly formulated. However, the review of the three areas of research discussed in this chapter points to questions of interest that were considered during the process of data collection and interpretation. Specifically, what is the nature and degree of extended family contacts among these geographically mobile families? If geographical distance reduces the supportive function of extended families, what, if any, social support systems are utilized instead? How do parents socialize their children in a community which is very different from the communities in which they grew up? These and related questions will be addressed in subsequent chapters.

Social scientists have the responsibility to state their value positions explicitly in order to aid their audience in interpreting their research. Should there be any confusion, this research was approached from the "cultural variant" perspective described earlier in this chapter. I agree with Pinderhughes's (1982) description of Afro-American families as influenced by 1) cultural residuals from Africa, 2) identification with mainstream America, and 3) responses to the "victim" system, i.e., racism and oppression. However, I recognize that families differ, based on different past and present family experiences, in the way in which they have been influenced by any of these three factors.

I intentionally chose not to use a control group, i.e., White families, for the study. Though the information generated from these family interviews may be of later usefulness to those interested in comparative family studies, my intention was *not* to see how closely these families approximate some White middle-class norm, so often the apparent purpose of studies involving Black families. My purpose was to try to understand the experience of these middle-class Black families living in a predominantly White community from *their* point of view. Surely the lives of Black families represent a subject that deserves attention for its own merits.

The usefulness of studying the family on its own merits has been demonstrated by other authors (Henry, 1965; Hess and Handel, 1959;

Rubin, 1976). Concern with norms and deviance has kept attention away from the very basic question of how families can differ in values and organization even within the same social segment of society. What makes a family the uniquely individual entity that it is?

The study of all families has not only been limited by its problem orientation, but also by its methodology. There has been an unfortunate mismarriage of clinical and experimental traditions which has dominated the field of family study (Bermann, 1973). As researchers attempted to quantify family interaction through laboratory studies with stringent controls, major gaps of information resulted. As Rubin (1976) aptly said, "We have probability statistics on marriage, divorce, sexual behavior, and much, much more; but they tell us nothing of the experience of the flesh-and-blood women and men who make up the numbers" (p.14).

The flesh-and-blood men, women, and children whose life stories make up the following chapters responded openly and frankly to the many questions that were asked. Although the interview questions were collectively broad in their scope, they were guided by three general questions. The first has already been stated: "In what ways do families vary, even within the same segment of society?" Encompassed in this question are, how does the family perceive itself and its mission, what tasks do they consider important, and how do they carry those tasks to their completion? The second question was, "What is the family's relationship to its history?" As upwardly mobile Black families, how did they perceive their own heritage and social context that is, for most, distinctly different from that of their families of origin? The third question was, "What is the family's relationship to the community?" Given the traditional pattern of Black families embedded in a support network of extended family and a larger Black community, how do these families perceive and respond to their nontraditional environment?

Of course, the responses to the questions that were asked did not always fall so discreetly into one of these three categories, just as the lives of the interviewed individuals cannot really be divided in this way. The conception of one's family is no doubt determined largely by one's view of his own history. How one evaluates the past certainly influences the view of the present. At the same time, new experiences in the present can color one's perception of the past. Although I shall proceed in a linear fashion through these three general topic areas, the reader is asked to think, if not read, in a circular fashion to see how these responses inform one another.

In a very real sense, as a Black woman who grew up in a predominantly White community, and now as a Black parent currently raising two children in such a community, I am a "participant-observer" in this research. As such, I share in the concerns expressed by some of these families. The recognized commonality in our situations doubtless opened family doors which might have remained closed. My experiences both as a Black child and as a Black adult living in a predominantly White environment increase my sensitivity to the experiences of the families in my sample. Hopefully, this sensitivity will enhance the reader's understanding of the data rather than hinder it.

Reading and re-reading the interview transcripts, I was certainly intrigued by them, not only as a researcher but as a Black parent myself, living in yet another predominantly White community. I believe the voices of the families of Sun Beach could be echoed in many barely integrated communities. For this reason, if no other, these "invisible families" need to be made visible.

2

Welcome to Sun Beach

E very town has something special, and Sun Beach is no exception. In fact, Sun Beach may have more "specialness" than most. With a population of approximately 75,000, it is a town large enough to call itself a city, yet is without the congestion, smog, or crime rate often associated with cities. The seat of Sun Beach County, this West Coast city boasts many cultural as well as physical attractions. Nestled between the ocean and the mountains, and connected by a major highway to two major cities, Sun Beach attracts thousands of visitors every year because of its natural beauty and easy accessibility.

Tourism is central to the Sun Beach economy. In addition, in the adjourning unincorporated area of Island View, non-polluting, high-tech research and development firms blessed with government contracts, and a university with approximately 18,000 students contribute to the economic health of the area. There are also two other smaller institutions for higher learning, as well as a technical school. Agriculture, in the outlying areas of the county, is another important revenue source.

All of these features, as well as the mild year-round climate and palm tree-lined streets, make Sun Beach not just a nice place to visit, but also to live. It is not uncommon to hear someone refer to Sun Beach as "Paradise." On the other hand, an unmarried Black woman once described it to me as "an ideal place only for newlyweds and nearly deads." From her point of view, the city was sadly lacking in eligible Black men, late night entertainment and cultural diversity in general. While not everyone seeks these qualities, there is no question that they are missing.

Though there is a significant Chicano population, a smaller Black population (2.4 percent), and a recent influx of Southeast Asian refugees, the community is predominantly White, and generally affluent. The largest "minority" group is not defined by race but by age. Roughly 20 percent of the population is over the age of 65, many of whom are quite wealthy and find Sun Beach to be a desirable retirement environment.

Families with children also see Sun Beach as a desirable environment, but unless a family has the resources to buy housing in a real estate market where the prices start well over $100,000, it is both difficult and expensive to find adequate housing. This situation is largely due to a building moratorium imposed in the mid-1970s to limit growth, conserve water, and to protect the general quality of life in the area. The political struggle between "no growth" environmentalists and eager developers is ongoing. Meanwhile, the shortage of affordable housing has led to a migration of low-income families out of Sun Beach.

Sun Beach is a city very conscious of its appearance, from the cleanliness of its beaches to the architectural design of the storefronts. Taking pride in its many examples of Spanish-style architecture, the city's Architectural Review Board must approve all new buildings and renovations in the downtown area to ensure that this tradition prevails.

In some ways, it seems that the city council's concern for appearances is echoed in the individual lifestyles of many of its residents. Health and fitness clubs abound, private and public hot tubs and jacuzzis are common, and self-improvement classes of all kinds are advertised. There are even tanning salons for those who do not want to lose that golden look during the rainy season. Sun Beach could easily be the origin of the California blond stereotype. While census figures do not reveal the percentages, the concentration of blue-eyed blonds (natural or otherwise) is apparent.

In this context, the resident Black population is in the unique position of being both very visible and very invisible simultaneously. Visibility comes from the small numbers; the occasional Black in the sea of blonds stands out. Yet there is no identifiable Black community, no street or neighborhood where it can be said, "That is where the Black people live." Instead the Black families are sprinkled like grains of pepper throughout the greater Sun Beach area. In one section of the city, the Hamill St. area, there is a higher concentration of low-income and working-class Chicano, White and Black families. But even this area does not have enough Black families in one place to characterize it as a Black neighborhood or community.

The following incident demonstrates the coexistence of the visibility and invisibility. A Black acquaintance was walking downtown one Saturday. He was approached by a Black couple who were apparently visiting Sun Beach. The couple asked him, "Where are all the Black folks? Don't they have any Black people around here?" Stopped because of his visibility, he was asked a question which addressed the invisibility of the Black community.

On another occasion, while dining in a restaurant, a Black busboy who cleared our table introduced himself, explained that he was new in town, and asked where he could get his hair cut. The availability of such mundane things as a barber trained to cut very curly hair, or of Afro-Sheen hair care products, or of greeting cards with dark faces can not be taken for granted. These goods and services are available, but one must know where to look.

While there are some Black civic and political organizations, some of those interviewed for this study questioned their effectiveness. Nevertheless, they represent attempts by a segment of the Black Sun Beach population to increase its political visibility. There is no doubt about the invisibility of the Black populous among elected officials in this politically conservative city. To date, none of the periodic attempts to elect a Black candidate to the Sun Beach city council have been successful. In the public schools, as in other areas of the community, the Black presence is barely noticeable. While two or three of the greater Sun Beach area schools can be identified as having a concentration of minority students, Black children, like their families, are sprinkled throughout the school system. There are only a handful of Black teachers.

But a town is made of more than its schools, its businesses, or its political structure. Families are the cement that holds a community together. The 10 families who participated in the interviews have all been a part of this community for at least 5 years. Some were educated here, some gave birth to their children here, some bought their first homes here. All work day-in and day-out to generate enough income to be able to stay here. Invisible though they may be, all have made a personal investment in this community.

Table 1 summarizes some of the demographic information about the participating families. All but 2 of the 20 adults interviewed have had some level of training beyond high school. Three of the wives were currently taking evening classes at the local community college. Five of the men have graduate degrees, including one doctorate. Three of these 5 mentioned during the interviews the possibility of returning to school to pursue doctorates themselves.

Table 1
Selected Characteristics of Participating Families

	Husbands N = 10	Wives N = 10
Age		
Range	32–52	29–47
Median	38	34
Education		
High school graduate	2	0
Some college or special training	2	4
College graduate	1	4
Graduate degree	5	2
Employment		
Employed full time plus second job	3	0
Employed full time plus school	0	3
Employed full time only	7	5
Employed part time	0	1
No paid employment	0	1
Years in Sun Beach		
Fewer than 5	0	0
6–10	4	5
11–15	0	1
Over 15	6	4
Region of origin		
North	0	1
South	5	5
West (other than Sun Beach)	2	2
Sun Beach	3	2

	Families N = 10
Income	
Range	28,000–50,000
Median	35,000
Numbers of children (at home)	
Range	1–3
Mean	1.9
Ages of children at home	
Range	0–14
Median	11

Though on the basis of income all of the families are middle-class, a great deal of family energy is expended to maintain that status. With the exception of 1 family, both spouses in all the families are employed outside the home. Three of the husbands also have part-time jobs, in addition to their full-time jobs, even though each of their wives is also working full-time. Six of the husbands are employed in white-collar positions, 3 of whom have supervisory responsibilities. Two of the 4 husbands in blue-collar positions have supervisory responsibilities.

That 9 of the 10 wives work outside the home is in keeping with the high level of Black maternal employment that has traditionally been a part of the economic survival of Black families. In fact, to be a working Black mother is so common that Peters (1976/1977) found that married Black women were surprised when she asked them, "Why do you work?" From the viewpoint of those mothers, who mainly worked for the money, a more appropriate or relevant question would have been, "Why don't you work?" Though I did not ask either question directly, based on their educational backgrounds and work history, the majority of the 9 women could be considered "career" employees, working toward, if not already occupying, professional positions. The one wife who was not employed apparently had the least economic need as her husband had the highest earnings in the group.

Eight of the 10 families were homeowners. As might be expected, the 2 renting families had the lowest incomes in the group.

Two of the families could be considered native to Sun Beach in that most of the childhood years of both sets of parents were spent in Sun Beach. One of the parents in a third family is also from Sun Beach, the spouse is from the South. In 4 of the families, both partners are from the South. The remaining adults were originally from either the Northeast or other parts of the West Coast. Five of the couples moved to Sun Beach together. The rest of them met their spouses in Sun Beach. With the exception of 2, all of the husbands' and wives' families of origin have their roots in Southern, typically rural environments, including those parents whom I have described as "native" to Sun Beach.

All of the households are nuclear. Five of the parents (4 fathers, 1 mother) had been previously married. With the exception of one of the husbands, all of the previously married spouses had children from these unions, however, none of these children currently lived with them. The children from these marriages are either over 18 and living away from home, or live elsewhere in the custody of their mothers. The average number of children for the present marriages was 1.9, ranging in age from newborn to 14 years old. Of the 19 children whose families were involved in the study, 15 were old enough to be interviewed.

Obviously, families are more than just the statistics that describe them. Knowing a person's name does not tell you who he/she is. Such knowledge comes from knowing the person's values and attitudes, goals and aspirations. It is in the personal articulation of these thoughts and feelings that a self is defined. The same could be said for a family. The lives of its members are woven with its goals, desires, dreams, and values. Inherent in the cloth is the family's own definition of what it should be, how it should function, its purpose for existing. How do these Sun Beach families define themselves?

DEFINING FAMILY VALUES

If you ask 20 different people what "family" means or what the main purpose of a family is, you will get 20 different answers, or so I thought. There are, after all, many ways to be a family. What was surprising to me was the similarity of response among the adults I asked. A family is togetherness, support, cooperation. It can be nuclear or extended in structure, but it is most often defined by its function rather than its form, as seen in the following examples:

> . . . a working unit where everyone within contributes to the total well-being of each individual . . . everyone took on part-time jobs, everyone did things to hold the family together.

> . . . togetherness, someone to respond to your needs, someone to share and enjoy life with, whether it is your immediate family or your ancestors.

And what are the most important functions of a family? Support, commitment and continuity are high on the lists of these men and women. "Sticking together," "working together," "just having some kind of security together"—mutual support is viewed as essential for both physical and emotional survival. One mother sums up this theme of mutual support in her own response to the question, "What is the *main* reason for a family?" She says:

> I think of things like acting as a supportive network for each other, and a sense of commitment to the individuals that make up that family. And that's something I grew up with and was communi-

cated from my own mother. Regardless of where you are or whatever they do, whether they be criminal or saint, there's a commitment to the well-being of that person. And I think the essence of what I believe about families is in that sense of commitment that you provide for the members.

The theme of continuity was expressed primarily in terms of the importance of children in a family. For example, one respondent comments:

> I think that families having children is important, because there is a sense of perpetuation, of the race, of the society . . . immortality.

Families (with children) are important to "carry on the family name," to "see oneself perpetuated." Continuity requires commitment, again to both physical and emotional survival. Children are a commitment to the future. One mother discusses her own sense of continuity in terms of training her children for that future:

> I think one of the main reasons for a family . . . is to perpetuate life and try to, as far as the children are concerned, rear them in such a way that they will want to make a contribution to society. I want them to move on and do what is necessary to make life better for the next generation.

Clearly children are important to these parents. But to talk about the importance of children after the fact of parenthood is perhaps to discuss the obvious. However, looking at the reasons why these adults chose to have children further highlights the significance of children in their lives and their conception of family. Even though all but one of these women work and most were educated to pursue careers of one sort or another, several expressed long-standing desires and/or expectations to be mothers. Said one, "I really just assumed I would have children. It never occurred to me that I would not."

Certainly in our society it is still expected that women will be mothers. So the fact that these women view motherhood as an inevitable part of their personal identity, and family identity, isn't really surprising. But this attitude toward parenting is not limited to women. The men also voiced long-held desires and expectations to raise children, as seen in the following example:

The fact of the matter is that I was raised with the understanding that our family is a family that has children, usually not a lot of children, but two or three children.

Of all the respondents, only one, an only child himself, expressed an original intention to remain childless.

This almost unanimous expression of the importance of children by both men and women suggests that the conclusion of others (Young, 1974; Nobles, 1976, 1978) about the value placed on children in Black families is correct. Nobles (1978) describes this value in family terms as a "child-centered system (the general organizational purpose of the family focuses on, if not requires, the presence of children)" (p.687). Certainly this statement could easily be made about these Sun Beach families.

It is generally acknowledged that the family is the primary transmitter of values to its children. One might expect that for families which could be described as child-centered, the family's role as a socializing agent would be taken very seriously. Although I did not observe these parents "in action" for other than brief encounters with their children, based on their responses to specific questions about values, rules and guidelines which should be communicated to children, all of these parents have strongly held beliefs about their children's family education. And the children, though generally less responsive to questions than their parents, reflect the adults' values about what it means to belong to a family. Two children, 12 and 13, provide these examples:

Well, to me, family means something that's together and doing things together, and love and care and happiness and giving things to people, and not just giving but receiving things . . . just a lot of doing things together.

The main reason for a family is to give shelter for one another. Love one another. Give each other support.

All families develop rules and guidelines, often unspoken which guide their interaction with one another. When asked about their own rules and guidelines, again a significant thread of commonality emerges. For 50 percent of the parents, the guiding family principle is respect, not only for self but for others, as exemplified by these comments:

I expect them to respect us at all times and respect each other, and we in turn do the same. We think it's very important to respect each other. There's a certain amount of minimal common courtesies that I think each family member deserves. A certain amount of respect.

We don't accept lying, we don't accept stealing, and we don't accept disrespect to grownups.

Another common, though less frequent, theme is that of shared responsibility. Of the 20 men and women, 7 talk about the importance of this in their families. Particularly since in almost all of the households both parents have paid employment, teamwork is essential for the family's successful functioning. As one woman says, "Everyone has to do something, so that we all can work." Her thoughts are echoed by this man:

A long time ago my wife and I established that there would be no boss in the house, that we would share that responsibility. . . . We've said to the kids. "This is our home." We're all responsible to maintain it. We all have a responsibility to take care of it, our home, and therefore everyone has a duty to perform, and if anyone needs help, we help him.

This theme of shared responsibility, though only mentioned by approximately one-third of the respondents in answer to this particular question, is an important one that emerges again in the context of educating children for their roles as men and women. Other themes which surface in response to this question, but are also discussed more fully in other contexts, are the importance of education, and religious values. Each of these will be elaborated upon later, in their own contexts. Another theme mentioned by 3 of the respondents, that of mutual support, is directly connected to the whole issue of what it means to be a family as it is defined by these participants. The following comment exemplifies the attitude expressed by these parents:

One of the things that I expect, and it even comes to disagreements with other children or wherever, I believe that they should protect and help each other . . . and they do that. I think it comes from the feelings we've projected to them in the past, and they have observed from me and my brother and sisters and my wife and her brothers . . . .I'm trying to demand that they stay close. I can't stand to see brothers and sisters being distant, I'm really a strong believer in that.

Collective survival means sticking together, helping one another out. To many of these parents, that is the essence of being a family.

SOCIALIZING THE CHILDREN

What one expects of family members at home may or may not be the same as what is expected when the family member is interacting with the outside world. Children are often a family's major link to the community. In child-centered families such as these, parents are quite aware that what children do or do not do out in the world is, at least in part, a reflection of their upbringing. As a result, they have clear ideas about how they want their children to conduct themselves, about how their children should be socialized. In this context, that of the child as the family's representative, certain family values become even more important.

The issue of respect is a case in point. As one father says:

> I want them to respect themselves, and how they present themselves to the people outside the family.... Respect is very important, not only of themselves but of the family, and be aware that what they do on the outside really has a bearing on us.

A mother expressed a similar sentiment, identifying this value as one that was passed on to her from her own parents. Carrying on the family tradition with her own added twist, she explains:

> Good manners I demand. I am probably less lenient about somebody using good manners than anything else probably I know ... respect is *very* high on my list. Also this is not just respect for adults, this is respect for your peer group too, but especially adults. Now this I'm sure I'm drawing from my folks because you had better respect older people when I was growing up. Today I don't feel it that strongly, because a lot of older people can take advantage of that.... I feel you have to earn respect. As children I have to teach you how to give it, but I also have to teach you how to earn it.

Another mother sees respect as the key to her children's success. Respect for yourself leads to the respect for and of others. Like the golden touch of Midas, it "radiates from you, and it doesn't matter what you touch."

In all, 15 of the 20 parents interviewed describe respect for self and others as one of the most important things they try to teach their children. Respect for others, particularly adults, has been described by others (Nobles, 1976; Mbiti, 1970; Peters, 1976/1977) as a value characteristic of African-American (as well as African) families. It is a value that is unmistakably present among this sample.

Although respect is by far the most commonly occurring theme, another related theme is the importance of self-confidence. Of course, self-confidence or self-esteem is important for every child, but it is clear that these parents understand that a Black child's sense of self-worth is often challenged by the sometimes hostile environment in which they must live. As one father explains:

> I try to help my children understand that they both have a certain amount of self-worth that's very important, very important, regardless of what the surrounding environment . . . might suggest.

Another father expressed similar sentiments in the very concrete terms of interacting with store clerks. He wants his children to walk with confidence, unintimidated, knowing that "as long as they got the money, they can have whatever they want."

Yet another father describes in broader terms his own diligent efforts to instill the necessary self-confidence and pride in his children. Setting time aside for "training sessions" with his two sons, he tries to impart some understanding of their cultural heritage as Blacks in America. For him, knowledge is power, and an empowered child will be a strong, effective adult. He elaborates:

> I was teaching them about Black culture, Black history, something about themselves, something about their heritage, and as we go along, some of the things they want to know is to . . . be able to assert themselves, to be able to stand up for what they believe, but not to be aggressive . . . that they have an identity of their own, and that they must walk in dignity. . . . I want them to understand what's been happening with Black people, the struggles that their mother and I were involved in, the struggles that some of our cultural heroes were involved in. One of my favorites is Frederick Douglass, and I'm anxious for them to get posters of people like him and put them on their wall instead of people like some of these rock heroes. My son is into the superheroes, and

I've been trying to convince him that he is his own superhero, and none of these superheroes, Superman, Spiderman, though they have supernatural powers, are more powerful than he is. And it's difficult because it is hard for him to understand what that is all about.

His wife offers her own explanation for why she feels the effort is necessary.

I'm a strong one for independence and individuality. I've always said I don't care what anybody else does, we do it this way . . . I think that's been a defense as much as anything else. And I've often wondered how I would have done things had I remained in my home town as opposed to here. . . . My son went to school where a lot of the kids were really quite wealthy and to me, he had a reason for being there and I wanted him to understand why he was there. And to understand that differences are just differences, so that he'd feel a sense of strength and confidence in himself as an individual, whatever outside trappings there might be. . . . I really have often asked myself how I would have reared my kids had we lived . . . where there is a Black population and where you learn a lot of things not through osmosis but something like that. . . . You begin to internalize values and perspectives because they're reinforced around you all the time. Your parents don't necessarily keep pouring them into you and banging them into you. So I have felt that it was important that the kids have a strong sense of who they are and that's as much because of the environment they're in, and because they are Black and in the environment they're in.

Listen to their voices and you will hear concern: concern for their children's developing racial identity. This is concern voiced by other parents as well. However, since so much of their thinking on the subject seems tempered by their perceptions of the community in which they are living, as evidenced by this last mother's remarks, the discussion of the development of racial identity must be delayed to be considered in the context of the family's relationship to Sun Beach itself.

Five of the parents mention the importance of education as one of the most important values they try to instill in their children, as represented by this father's response:

I'm very strong when it comes to education. That's one of the things about me. I always felt that this was the only true freedom for the Black person, through education, and therefore I had to enforce this and be very strong about this with my children. I didn't tolerate bad grades in school because I felt that most of my education I had to get part time and receive certain type of grades and deal with the stress and strain of an eight-hour-a-day job, then it should be obvious to anybody that if you just spend a third of the time allotted to you in your studies, you could do just as good.

This father struggled for the education he received. He now demands that his children put effort into their own. Another father also insists on his children's academic effort. He states:

The main thing that I'm asking them to do is to study, and get their homework done, get good grades. We really get down on them . . . 'cause I know they need education. See, they don't know they need it, but I know. My father didn't push me the way I'm pushing them. I wish he had.

Although only 25 percent of the respondents identify the value of education as one of the most important lessons they try to teach their children, when specifically asked about the issue of education, all of the parents indicate that educating their children is very important to them. As parents of upwardly mobile families, success—their own and/or that of their children—is a topic to which they frequently refer. With little, if any, accumulated wealth to pass on to their children, they recognize that to a large extent their children will have to pave their own way. The education they receive then becomes that much more important. Says one father:

I don't have a business in which my girls can work, so once they get out of high school, they have to be educated so that they can go to work. Like most kids whose parents own businesses, like at the university, they don't need to worry about it too much, they know that they're going to be taken care of, but I don't have that insurance at all. So definitely they got to be educated. Definitely. Definitely.

The quality of the education that their children receive is at least as important as the quantity. In fact, one mother admits that the subject of her children's education has sometimes caused her considerable distress. Yes, she believes that education is the only hope her children have of "getting anywhere." But unless it is a "good education," defined as "one that will teach them how to function," it will be of little use.

Although education is highly valued by all, there is variation in the way quality is defined and the degree to which parents are willing to sacrifice to provide it. For some, quality education means finding the best public school you can find. For others, it means finding the best school you can find, public or private, regardless of the cost. A few of the parents speak of personal and/or financial sacrifices they have made to ensure the high quality of their children's education. For example, one father describes a decision he made to give up a job and their "dream house" in another community to return to Sun Beach, primarily because he felt the public schools in Sun Beach were better. Parents from two other families mention the financial sacrifices they have made to send their children to an excellent, but very expensive, private school. Another mother expresses very clearly that her children's education is important to her, but it will not be handed to them on the proverbial silver platter. She explains:

> I will try to gear them toward college and hope that they can make it there. . . . I think I owe them four years of college. . . . Beyond that whatever they can help themselves with, I want to help them too. But they will have to help themselves after four years. This means med school, law school, whatever. And it can be done, I know. I'm drawing from experience because it was very rough when we grew up, very, very rough. And my kids will have to know the importance of things they want and how to get them, but they're not going to be handed to them. That may be strict but that's me.

Again the children have clearly heard and understood their parents' messages about the importance of education. All of the children interviewed indicate that they like school. When asked about the importance of completing school, both boys and girls unanimously respond that completing their education is important.

The emphasis on education in these families is consistent with other studies of Black families (Billingsley, 1968; Peters, 1976/1977; Hines and Boyd-Franklin, 1982). Hill (1971) has identified this value as one of the strengths of Black families.

Another strength identified by Hill (1971) and others is the emphasis that Black families have traditionally placed on the importance of religion. Given this historical context, it is interesting to note that only 2 of the 20 parents mentioned religious values as among the most important ones to teach their children. However, based on their reports of weekly activity, 4 of the families attend church together regularly. The issue of the role of religion in the family is one to which we shall return in the context of the discussion of the respondents' families of origin.

An important aspect of any child's socialization is understanding what it means to be a man or a woman. How do these Black mothers and fathers feel their sons and daughters should be socialized in this regard? This topic is of particular interest given the much debated issue of what has alternately been described negatively as female dominance (Frazier, 1939; Moynihan, 1965; Rainwater, 1966) or more positively, as egalitarian and flexible sex-role relationships (Scanzoni, 1971; Hill, 1971; Peters, 1976/1977) within Black families. When asked if there is anything special sons/daughters should be taught, half of the parents indicate that they try not to make a sexual distinction between their children. What is important for one to know is also important for the other. For example, one mother comments:

> I try not to do any special things for him because I don't want him to grow up expecting something different, nor do I want her to expect something different . . . this will help both of them. For example, I don't want him to feel that because he's a man he must not cry or be expected to not have any failures or expect someone to take care of him. And with my daughter it's much the same.

Her husband, however, is typical of some of the respondents who initially indicated that they did not make a distinction but then qualified their remarks in various ways. For example:

> I guess if there were some distinction, I don't want to sound like a chauvinist but I really want my son to be very dependable. I want him to acquire a great deal of discipline. I would say we try to teach that same thing to my daughter but to a lesser degree.

The theme of male responsibility is echoed by 11 of the parents. Fathers, especially, seem to emphasize this point. Of the 10 fathers interviewed, 7 elaborate on it, particularly in terms of sexual responsibility and responsibility to support one's family. Or as one father puts it, "Don't just go get kids to be getting kids." Understanding the financial responsibility of fatherhood is stressed.

Mothers are more likely to also emphasize the need for sons to be able to assume responsibility in the home. Boys should know how to cook, to clean, to do all the things "you would normally teach girls." However, the issue of household responsibilities is not expressed only by the mothers. One father is quite to the point in his comment:

> I try to teach them all the same, because a girl can be a mechanic just as good as a boy . . . or a man can cook just as good as a woman as far as I'm concerned. I'll get on the kitchen table with any woman myself because I cook for a hobby. I teach them all to make their beds and clean their rooms, so to me that's not a man's job or a woman's job, that's a person's job.

Another father describes how he gets his point across through his own actions. His son sees him meeting his own responsibilities, going to work everyday, returning home to his family each night, and doing his share of the housework. In this way, his son is "learning what it is to be a man, what the male role is to be." Similarly a mother describes the importance of her husband's example in communicating this message. Her son will not grow up "expecting a wife to cook, clean and everything," because that is not how his family does things. Her husband, who routinely cooks at least one meal a day, is an important role model for him.

This attitude toward the socialization of sons is consistent with the theme of shared responsibility expressed in the earlier discussion of the meaning of family and seems to support the view that egalitarian sex-role relationships are valued, particularly in middle-class Black families (Willie and Greenblatt, 1978). Based on the responses of this sample, it seems that that value is shared by both men and women.

Thus far, this discussion has been centered on the socialization of sons. Is there anything special these parents want to teach their daughters? The answer is yes. Of those parents who indicate any sexual distinction in the treatment of their children, the major theme is female independence and assertiveness. They want their daughters to know how to take care of themselves. As one mother says, "life is hard," and a woman who is totally dependent on a man is at risk. Self-reliance is seen as an essential form of life insurance for developing Black women.

Fathers, as well as mothers, emphasize the importance of their daughters' self-reliance. The fathers' responses are of particular interest since it is the Black male who has been the alleged victim of Black female assertiveness. One father explains:

> They got to know how to take care of themselves. I know that guys need to know this, too, but more so I think with females, because they can be vulnerable to a lot of things.

Another father elaborates on this point even further:

> There's not a lot of difference between boys and girls as far as responsibility is concerned, but the strongest thing I think any parent should teach a girl is to be self-supporting, be independent. . . . It's a threat to some men, but to a real man, I don't see how it can be. I still stress it with my girls. Nothing wrong with you quitting your job or relieving yourself of your duties on a job to have your children or whatever, but the idea of being self-supporting is that . . . so much stress and strain that you don't ever have to be subjected to . . . Live with a man because you love and respect him, not because of fear of economic reasons. You've got to be able to deal with that prior to even getting married, and the only way you know for a fact is that you've got to prove to yourself that you can do it. Because if you don't, there's always going to be that fear, that you can't make it without him. That ain't necessarily true. I think it's important for a girl to know.

Apparently these fathers not only are not threatened by the idea of their daughters' independence, but they also encourage it. This attitude is consistent with their comments about the need for both sexes to be educated. Lewis (1975, p. 228) wrote that Black children are not socialized with "standards that polarize behavioral expectations according to sex." As with the families Lewis described, it would appear that the majority of these families use overlapping categories for what is gender appropriate behavior rather than mutually exclusive ones.

Despite what seems to be a trend toward healthy androgyny, while comparing the responses of husband and wives, I noticed an apparent divergence in opinion on this subject in a couple of families. Below are the responses of one of these husband-wife pairs. The wife outlines a plan for preparing her daughter for corporate success, while her husband sounds as though he is training her for the role of "happy homemaker."

> *Wife*: I think it's important for her to . . . take leadership roles . . . just making sure that she is thinking. And I guess I'm going under the assumption too that usually men are expected to think, men are expected to work on teams, and are expected to do those types of things that I want to instill in my daughter, because usually women are perceived as not having those qualities. But my expectation is that my son by osmosis will have those qualities.

> *Husband*: Okay . . . I think the thing that I'm trying to teach her is to be a supporter of the family, to be understanding, be sensitive, be loving, be feminine. . . . These kinds of things are very, very important.

This husband's view initially seems to be quite different, if not actually in opposition, to that of his wife. But as he continues in his comments, the two parents seem less far apart. He adds:

> I just don't want anybody to hold her back. She can be whatever she wants to be, and she'll have our support. Number one, respect yourself and others will respect you, strive to understand things that are happening in your own environment, and be a lady. I think she should be a lady.

Another husband has a similar message for his daughter: "Be feminine-like," while his wife advises her "to get out there and fight for yourself, because nobody else is going to do it for you."

Are these husbands and wives actually in disagreement about the socialization of their daughters? Are the fathers at least partially in favor of stereotypically female roles for their daughters, while their wives are more clear-cut in their support for an assertive stance? Although it might seem so initially, an alternate interpretation may be that these parents are expressing different aspects of a similar expectation, that is, the expectation that their daughters, like the wives in these families, will perform in a dual capacity as homemakers and wage earners.

Children learn not only from what their parents say but also from what their parents do. Certainly the children in these families see their mothers performing this dual function (with the exception of the one wife who is not employed outside the home). They also see their fathers supporting their mothers in that capacity and performing their own dual function at home and at work. Describing his own activity in this context, one father comments:

> One of the things my kids see me do is share. . . . I don't care what people think . . . I will vacuum, I will dust, I will wash windows, I will iron clothes, and I do. . . . When it comes to ironing the kids' school clothes, if she has papers from the office that she's working on . . . I will go to ironing. . . . It's a small way of showing appreciation, but any way of showing appreciation helps. . . . That's the way I saw my grandparents, so that's the way I am.

Like this father, another man is living out the patterns of his own socialization as a child. In his own way, he is a testimony to the power of his own father's example, saying:

> I get up, I cook the breakfast for the kids . . . make the lunches, and make sure that everybody's getting up and moving. Not to say that my wife won't do those things, but basically I'm an early riser, a mover. The way I was raised my dad . . . spent more time in the kitchen. He was the one that actually got things moving. . . . It's kind of funny, I used to criticize him when I was living at home about . . . washing dishes and cooking and doing these things that were primarily women's work, but not to know that I was going to be doing those things myself.

The role of fathers in the socialization of their children deserves particular emphasis, given the tendency of many studies of Black families to either ignore the presence of the father or to suggest that his role is a peripheral one, as has been noted by Allen (1981), J. McAdoo (1981), and Cazenave (1979), as well as others. The fathers in this sample are directly involved in their children's lives on a daily basis (with the exception of one father whose work takes him out of town for several days at a time). For some that may mean transporting their kids to and from school, checking their homework, or preparing breakfast in the morning or dinner in the evening. For some it includes going with their children to church, taking them shopping on weekends, or watching them participate in athletic or other extracurricular events. The particular nature of their interaction is prescribed in large part by their working hours. But the commitment to parenthood is very definitely a joint one in these families.

For these Sun Beach families, family life means children, mutual support, togetherness, and shared responsibilities. They describe their own families in those terms. "Very close" is a description commonly used. One father sums it up like this:

> This family is really pretty good. I . . . stressed the need to care
> for one another, the importance of it, and support for each other's
> ideas and thoughts. By doing this you can actually achieve a lot
> of things which you couldn't do by yourself, and that itself I feel
> I have accomplished through my kids. I see a lot of this being
> accomplished through my father's people. It was more or less a
> traditional type thing that I wanted to carry over to my children.
> You can always have one that's not as supportive as the others,
> but all in all I think they're pretty much on target on the things
> that I consider as a family.

But all is not perfect in the "paradise" known as Sun Beach. When both parents work, sometimes more than one job, there is not always enough time for family, for children. There does not seem to be enough time for togetherness, one father laments:

> In terms of spending time with my family, that's one of the things
> that really has bothered me. Number one, I have outside interests,
> and the kids have a lot of outside interests, and as a family we
> don't spend as much time as we should. . . . My wife has meetings
> to attend . . . my kids have plans on the weekends. . . . We're
> always going off in different directions, and one of the things I
> was going to try to do was try to spend more time with them.

It is in situations like these that extended family members have often helped to fill in the gaps left by over-committed parents, providing support and assistance to both parents and their children. But most of these families are without immediate physical access to this kind of familial support. Nevertheless, the question of the role of extended family in the lives of these parents and their children is still an important one. Inasmuch as extended family members represent the families of origin, they become a link to these husbands' and wives' past—a past which, upon examination, hopefully will shed more light on the nature of the present for these parents and their children.

3

A Long Way from Home

For someone from a small Southern town or an East Coast city, this California coastal community literally is a long way from home. But distance can be measured in more than just miles, and even those born and raised in California, or even other parts of Sun Beach, might feel a long way from the places of their childhood. After all, the question, "Where are you from?" can have as much to do with psychology as it does geography.

Table 2 summarizes some of the demographic characteristics of the participants' families of origin. Geographically speaking, the overwhelming majority of these families have their roots in Southern, mostly rural communities. They grew up during a time period when legally sanctioned segregation was the order of the day. That fact in itself places these Sun Beach families in a very different social context than that of their families of origin. In addition, they have a much higher level of education as a group than their parents had. While all but 2 of the participants have had some educational training beyond high school, slightly more than half of their parents never made it to high school. Children of what most described as working-class families, they now describe themselves as middle-class. Raised in households full of children (half had 6 or more siblings), their own households barely average 2 children per family.

Unquestionably the demographic differences between one generation and the next are considerable. How much distance has been placed between that past and this present? To what extent are the themes of one generation echoed in the next? Retrospectively, how do these men and women view their own upbringing? The participants were asked to discuss various aspects of their early home life, including how money, housework, education, religion, and recreation were

Table 2
Selected Characteristics of Participants' Families of Origin

	Mothers N = 20	Fathers N = 20
Region of origin		
North	1	1
South	17	17
Midwest	0	0
West	2	2
Rural	11	11
Small town	7	7
Urban	2	2
Level of education		
No formal education	1	1
Elementary school (K–6)	5	3
Jr. high school (7–9)	3	8
High school (10–12)	7	6
Trade school	2	0
Business school	0	1
College graduate	1	1
Graduate school	1	1

	Families N = 20
Social class	
Upper class	0
Middle class	4
Working class	15
Lower class	1
Number of children	
Range	1–13
Mean	6.5

handled within the family. The following is a sampling of some of the men's recollections.

One man, raised in California, recounts:

> We lived in the poor part of town, but I can remember statements made by my grandmother and grandfather, "You'll always have plenty to eat." I've never seen them unable to come up with the bail money, lunch money, the new clothes, the new shoes . . . but I can remember when they had to struggle to get $15 because I wanted some Adidas. . . . I saw my grandfather go cut three lawns . . . to get me those shoes. He didn't put a dime in his pocket, and he had just got off another job. So to me, that's what I saw, a hell of a lot of love.

After the sudden death of his mother, a young woman still in her 20s, his grandparents "gave up their lives" to help his overwhelmed father hold his family together. Their struggle provided an object lesson in collective survival that he will never forget.

Education and religion were both very important in his grandparents' household. Everyone in the family was very proud when his sister graduated from college, and perhaps disappointed when he and his brother did not. Religious education was emphasized, and the church played an important supporting role in family life. Laughing, he says:

> We *stayed* in church, we did. We were ushers, in choirs, it was a very important part of our family structure. . . . They reared us really in the church, and I think that's also true again of most Black families.

It was certainly true of a Southern-born man, raised in a family of 12 children. He recalls:

> Well, we had a whole lot of religion . . . when we were real young, my dad certainly tried to impress upon us the value of religion, the value of Christianity, the value of living a good life. . . . He expected you to go to church regularly and expected you to participate in the various services. He was a very strong Sunday school person. He had a real thirst for education although he didn't finish high school. . . . So he felt, I think, that the Sunday school was the most intellectual part of the whole activity. . . . He insisted that his children become in-

volved in Sunday school where they would study the Bible and other related books to learn as much as they could about the history of religion and so forth.

Although he has only two children of his own, he remembers life in a large family as "the greatest experience I could have had," and though they never had a lot of money, "it was a very happy, very good experience." With such a large family, everyone had to pitch in. A collective effort was required for family survival, a fact the children simply accepted. He recalls:

> Five or 6 of us went and picked cotton for a week.... At the end of the day, my dad would say, "Well, I think this week, boys, we need to turn that money into the general fund." Except maybe you could keep a dollar or something like that to go and buy yourself some candy or whatever.... The money we made became family money. The same was true when you worked on your job.... You were expected to make some kind of contribution to the running of the family ... that was something that was taught and I don't think anybody resented that very much.

Here, too, education was highly valued. All the children were expected to go to school and to do well there. In fact, after each of the three oldest children decided to go to a college in another part of the state, his financially drained father, unwilling to deny them this educational opportunity, demonstrated his commitment to his children's education by making an important decision:

> My dad said, "Look, this is crazy for me to be paying all that tuition and all that board." So ... he sold his house ... and bought a house right off the campus, where anybody who wanted to go to school could just go. You'd stay at home and you'd just pay $60 a semester.... I think that was one of the most significant moves we made, as far as we were concerned.

Not all of their parents had such a high level of commitment to their children's education. One man, from a family of 13, found his own formal education cut short when his father became disabled. As the oldest boy, he had to leave school when he was still in the tenth grade to help support his brothers and sisters.

This man, who ultimately did return to school, learned early what it meant to be responsible, not just as a breadwinner but in all areas of family life.

> With all of them sisters I had, you would think I was exempt from any household work at all, but my mother had the attitude that if I was going to grow up to be a healthy man, I had to learn to cook, I had to learn to sew, everything the girls learned, I had to learn it. . . . She said, "Well, you're going to learn it because you might have to someday do it for yourself."

They, too, "stayed" in church. His father insisted on it. He explains:

> You didn't get too grown to go to church and Sunday school, no matter what age you were. Two things you didn't do was play ball and fish on Sunday, and I liked to do both of them. . . . If you stayed in his home, you just simply dealt with religious activities, you didn't question it, that's all. . . . I always said that when I got on my own, I'd never go back to church.

To forego a game of baseball or an afternoon of fishing on a Sunday must have been a hard thing for a young boy to do, especially since life on a farm offered little time for recreation. Whether it was feeding the horses or milking the cows, there was always something that had to be done, seven days a week. Yet despite the work, the early hardships, and educational sacrifices, life with 12 brothers and sisters was "fun." The good times created a bond of closeness that has lasted through the years.

These responses are typical of most of the other descriptions given by the men in the sample. Although their families may have struggled financially, these men recount generally pleasant memories of their own upbringing. Even in hard times, children can experience happiness.

But sometimes, the times are just *too* hard. It is indeed a long way from a one-room house on a Southern dirt road to the comfort and convenience of a Sun Beach subdivision. Although there may have been joyful moments for him and his 7 brothers and sisters, another respondent looks back and focuses on the bleakness of his childhood. He says:

> It was like sardines in a can. It was that way. We had a one-room house, and then we expanded to another room. So three sleeping in a bed . . . not having a bathroom, not having all the conveniences you would have in a modern home. We struggled, the clothes

we had to wear, you had to make ends meet the best way you
could. It was a total experience. That was really something else.
But that's life.

When I ask how the family handled money problems, he, laughing
wryly, responds:

Money problems? I'll tell you about money problems. We had
very little of it, so we had very few problems. The thing was since
we were working on the farms, what was grown, we'd eat that. If
it was cabbage season, we were cutting cabbage and we'd eat
cabbage five days a week. When bean season was on, we'd eat
beans five days a week. Whatever was in season, that's what
you'd eat. We raised hogs, put the meat up and it'd last us all
winter. Then you could always buy canned goods and put them
under the bed and when it got real cold and you couldn't do
anything, just open up canned goods. . . . There was no squabble
over money, definitely no squabble because there was none. . . .
When my stepfather used to make any money, he would bring it
home and give it to my mother. He couldn't read or write, about
all he could do was count money.

The struggle for economic survival was followed closely by a striving
for spiritual survival. *Every* Sunday was spent in church. As he puts it,
"That was the law." But education was a lower priority.

My parents weren't educated. They couldn't teach us anything.
. . . If we didn't learn it from teachers at school, we had to
figure it out ourselves. We didn't have anybody at home that
could explain it to us, except my older brother who was pretty
smart. We helped each other. . . . My stepfather felt the schools
weren't teaching us anything. He didn't know because . . . he
never went to school a day in his life.

Although his mother wanted her children to have an education, the
labor of strong teenage boys was a valuable family resource which had
to be utilized. Going to school became a subject for negotiation and
compromise.

Some days we would have to stay out because he would put too
much pressure on her for us to stay out because he's promised the

White man, "Hey, I'll have my boys over here tomorrow." So, okay, he'd made a commitment to the man to get us there. . . . I'd say I wanted to go to school. . . . Mom would say, "Y'all can go to work tomorrow, and go to school the next day." So we'd do that, and we went through high school like that, our whole life, maybe staying out a couple of days, going to school maybe three, and so forth, to make money so we could buy our clothes and help with the bills.

It is a testimony to a mother's encouragement, receptive teachers, and their own talent that, despite sporadic school attendance, at least three of the children (including this man) made it to college and beyond.

For all of these men, there is no question that at least the physical circumstances of their lives have changed a great deal since their youth. When asked if there is a difference between their current family practices and those of their families of origin, the responses are mixed. For the last respondent, the two seem worlds apart. Everything is different, just as he hoped it would be. With determination in his voice, he answers:

Definitely very different . . . when you live in a place with no electricity, no indoor restrooms, no shower, holes in the walls, roof leaking every time it rains, definitely I was looking to get me a better place of my own. . . . That was my number one goal, to get away from there and do better than what they were doing. . . . I did, I got out of there. It worked out that I could get out of the situation.

For others, perhaps there are more similarities than differences. One man, who himself works two jobs, says:

Well, when you see your parents work four and five jobs just to keep food on the table during their times and the economic situations and the racial problems that they incurred, that's the reason that I struggled so hard to make sure that when I had a family that I was going to try and . . . follow in the pattern of my grandparents, my father, to give them the necessities, even if I had to work as hard as they did. Like my grandfather and my father always told me, "We tried to do the best we could for you, and the only thing we ask of you is to do better by yours." And that's what I'm trying to do.

Another man acknowledges that social and economic changes allow him to provide things for his children that his parents were not able to provide for him. His son can be involved in athletic activities that might formerly have been "only for White folks." He and his wife can support these activities with both their time and their money in a way that his parents could not. Yet these increased opportunities have not changed his basic values. They are still very similar to those of his parents. Religion is still "a part of the family culture, family trait, family need," and education is a high priority for his children. Summing up the continuity of values in his own family, one father says:

> If you are asking me did the way I was raised have anything to do with the way I raise my children, to a great extent it did. . . . We was a poor family, we didn't have a lot of money. We didn't have the best style of clothes or flashy cars or this type of thing, but . . . we did care about each other and we were taught to respect ourselves and other people, and we were taught there were certain things we just don't do. As a result of all this sheer teaching and discipline . . . I look back over the years of my life growing up in those areas and realizing the respect some of those people still have for me, I feel quite proud that I was raised that way.

The descriptions that several of the women in the sample give of their childhood experiences are not unlike those described by the men, as seen in the following example. Like most of the men, this woman grew up in a family in which religion and education were emphasized. Like others, her family struggled financially. However, for this woman, the fact of their poverty was a realization made in adulthood. It had not been a part of her consciousness as a child. She observes:

> We all lived there, my mother, my father, my grandmother, and seven children . . . and two cousins. But I never thought of it as being crowded, or cramped, or poor. We always had plenty to eat. I can't ever remember being hungry as a child. I don't ever remember needing anything and not having it, so I never thought about money.

As in most of the other families, everyone had duties to perform, including attending both school and church.

My mother felt very strongly about education. To her horror, she has one child that dropped out of school. She sent us to school and expected us to do well. . . . Her feeling was if you go to school and you pay attention, you'll learn and if you're learning what you're supposed to be learning, you'll get good grades. To her, it was just as simple as that. . . . Everybody went to church on Sunday, whether you wanted to or not. My mother has a rule, "It doesn't make any difference how old you are, as long as you live under my roof, you go to church on Sunday. Now if you go out on Saturday night and you stay out until 10:30 Sunday morning, you had better be in church at 11:00." That's the way it was, that's how it is.

Three of the 10 women describe their families of origin as middle-class, as opposed to only one of the men. As the saying goes, "Money isn't everything," but it definitely can make a difference. The impact of improved economic conditions is apparent in their descriptions of their own childhoods. Commenting on her life of relative comfort in a small Southern town, one woman says:

I thought I was rich . . . until I went away to college. I didn't do a lot of housework. . . . My father cooked, he helped around the house, but my brother and I didn't do a lot. . . . It was always assumed that we would go away to school . . . that we would go to college. We didn't go to church that often.

Another woman, her perspective influenced by the fact of 10 brothers and sisters, also describes a financially stable existence:

We never experienced having money problems because we always had everything. . . . Even when I graduated from college, it wasn't hard because I got out of school, three weeks later I had a job. . . . I got a car from my aunt, a brand new car for a graduation present, so you know I had everything. . . . I started off making $8,000 a year, so that was big money for a young college graduate back in the early seventies, and when I would spend up all my money, I would just call my parents and tell them I needed some money and they helped me out. That was never a problem. But when I got married, my husband was a student and not being able to have was a real hard adjustment. . . . In our family of 11 kids, all of us went to college except 4 of us. . . . We all went to church every Sunday. . . . I always said I would never go when I got grown . . . because I remember there were times when we didn't want to go, but we had to.

For these women, the difference between the economic contexts of their childhood and adulthood is less marked, though certainly having both lived in the South with the social norm of segregation, they have experienced environmental changes. Yet they see their children's experiences as basically very similar to their own.

While growing up in a middle-class home meant life was easier in some ways, there does not seem to be that much difference between any of the families in terms of the values stressed. In almost all, education was seen as very important by at least one, if not both, of the parents, though families varied in their ability to translate their desire for education into the actual achievement of it. In all but one of the families of origin, religious participation was heavily stressed. The role flexibility of men and women was evident in most of the families as their mothers and fathers shared in the financial and domestic maintenance of their homes. Although most emphasized by those respondents from large families, the themes of mutual support and shared responsibility were also evident.

It appears that the socialization practices of the participating parents are well rooted in their own family traditions. The variations that exist among those traditions seem to be more in terms of degree of emphasis rather than direction of emphasis.

It is a long way from a mother's grade-school education to a daughter's college education. One woman who has crossed this distance points out how the difference of degree in emphasis on education between herself and her husband derives from variance in their backgrounds, and how this difference is translated into their actions. She explains that her husband is "more relaxed about education" than she is, but that his family has had access to education in a way that hers has not. His mother has a college education, her mother did not finish elementary school. As she says, "If you don't have it, somehow it seems bigger."

Though clearly they both want quality education for their children, it is she that has insisted on keeping them in an expensive private school, even when family finances were stretched to their limit. In light of this mother's comments, it is interesting to point out that among the 4 families that have children enrolled in private schools, at least one of the spouses is from a family where a parent had less than a seventh grade education.

Though there has clearly been continuity from one generation to the next, there has also been change. One such pattern of change is the shift in religious practice from one generation to the next. As previously mentioned, church involvement was a required part of family life in almost all of the families of origin, but only 4 of the 10 families in this sample attend church on a regular basis. Ironically, the 2 respondents who mentioned they would never go to church again once they left home are represented among the 4 church-going families.

Since most of the adults grew up in churches with predominantly Black congregations, one might think that the decline in attendance is due to lack of interest in membership in a church of another denomination or with a predominantly White congregation. However, this explanation seems unlikely since, despite the small size of the Black population, there are several churches with predominantly Black congregations representing an assortment of denominations in Sun Beach.

Several of the respondents, commenting on the fact that they are no longer actively involved in organized religion, gave a variety of reasons for the change in the level of their participation, ranging from a general loss of interest in organized religion to a desire to sleep late on Sunday.

However, the shift away from organized religion is not necessarily a shift away from spirituality. As one woman explains:

> I'm just not involved in religion. . . . I haven't been involved for probably 16 or 18 years. . . . My concern is that the kids have a moral perspective and some values. . . . I would not like to see the kids highly ritualize their religion. I would like to see it more internal than that.

Whatever the reason, it is a shift away from a particular support network and source of socialization that they had as children. In this sense, the change represents a loss for their own children now growing up in Sun Beach. When the former significance of the church as an institution in the parent's own lives is acknowledged, the significance of this loss can be clearly seen.

Several of the parents do recognize that the church as an institution was more than just a place of worship in their communities. For some, church activities were a source of recreation, and opportunities for positive social interaction. Even the woman whose parents had not heavily emphasized church attendance found the social environment a powerful magnet in her adolescence. She often attended church with her best friends' family "not only for the religious aspect, but for the social aspect."

The church provided social support for whole communities. Says one man, "In my area, people was really tied up in the church. . . . That had a major role in keeping Black families together." Another describes the supportive role of the church in terms of the personal relationships that were fostered there. There was the minister himself, a "fabulous old guy," and there was the "extremely nice" couple he sat next to every Sunday. They would occasionally buy him a youth membership at the YMCA. He remembers, "People like that were very supportive of me when I was small."

Perhaps the increased recreational opportunities in an environment like Sun Beach offset the social function of the church, and perhaps the generally improved economic status of the families lessens the need for the support the church can provide in times of economic hardship. Certainly any of these parents could afford to buy their children YMCA memberships themselves if they chose to do so.

Nevertheless, the loss of this particular support network for the majority of the sample families seems particularly significant if coupled with the loss of other informal community support networks and extended family networks, which embraced these adults when they were growing up. The following excerpts provide examples of how these networks operated back then from the viewpoint of 2 of the women:

> When I look back, even when I look back a few years, when I was a teenager, I never realized how poor we were. I figured we had shelter, we had food, we had clothes, we had family. I wondered what else you needed really. . . . We had a garden, we'd kill hogs and everybody would share in the meat. . . . The guys would go deep-sea fishing, and everybody would have a community bonfire . . . and share in the wealth they had caught. . . . Recreation included church activities, going to the beach, or going to the lake . . . or going with some family or two in the car, because we didn't have a car. . . . My dad's younger brother was very good about doing that, . . . coming to take us out on special outings.

Though surely special to its residents, this community was not unique. In another town, in another state, the sounds of community spirit were being echoed:

> We didn't do a lot of going to Disneyland type of things because, now I realize, we didn't have the money . . . so most of our recreation involved eating. And of course, we lived in a neighbor-

hood where everybody was a part of the family. Everyone was just one big family, the whole street, . . . recreation was often-times getting together the neighborhood, Saturday fishfries, and those types of things.

Sharing similar memories, both remember the important contribution members of their communities made to the social and economic well-being of their own families.

Other respondents particularly emphasize the role of extended family members in their social network. For example:

We're stereotyped as being workers, no time for recreation unless the father went out on the weekend drinking and the mother stayed at home doing the work. But we never did that, and that's why I tell my kids, we always did things together. My parents were always together, on every issue from the recreational aspect to the discipline, the whole social aspect, everything! . . . Every Saturday, we did grocery shopping. It was a family thing, and after that we'd come home and we'd just play with the little nieces and nephews and cousins. . . . Then on Sundays we'd go visiting our grandparents . . . or we'd have visits from our older sisters and their families, and we'd go to the Botanical Gardens . . . we went to the beach together, everything was always family.

Although only 4 of the 20 adults had extended family members living with them when they were children, almost all had frequent contact with at least some of their relatives.

For many of the respondents, it was these extended family contacts that gave them a sense of family history and strengthened their family as well as their racial identity. Important messages were embedded in the family stories that grandparents, aunts, and uncles, as well as their own parents, told most of them when they were growing up. For example, one of the men describes the influence of family stories on his current attitudes.

My dad and my grandad emphasized, at least they talked very much about how difficult it was for them to survive and earn a living. They talked so much about that . . . I think that had some bearing on me and my interest in trying to get a fairly decent education so I would not have to be struggling to survive economically. Some of the other problems are pretty much the

same or in worse shape than they were fifty years ago. Some of
the racism . . . is more sophisticated but it's still there. But I think
one means of upward mobility, one means of surviving at a
different level or reasonably comfortable level is to emphasize
trying to get the best education we can. I think the chances will
be that you will be able to live a little better life if that should
occur. So I guess that's probably been transmitted to me, and I
hope to do that for my kids.

For him, preparing oneself to deal with racism, in this instance through
educational achievement, was an important family message. Others also
got messages on this subject from their extended family members. As
one man recounts:

When my mother was a child, she and her dad went into town in
one of those old wagons. I guess they were at a general store, and
my grandfather was buying some items. Upon leaving, one of the
guys called him a "nigger," and my grandfather actually got down
off his wagon and just beat this guy to a pulp. . . . My mom really
prides herself on letting us know the type of man my grandfather
was . . . she prides herself on letting us know that my grandfather
actually did something about a statement that was being directed
against the family.

To have an ancestor brave enough to confront a White oppressor is
an obvious source of pride, especially since such acts almost always had
dangerous, if not life-threatening, implications. Such confrontations did
not always take the form of overt physical challenges. One woman gives
an example of covert action, a secret mission carried out by her
grandfather which ultimately benefitted the entire Black community in
which he lived.

They all lived on this plantation. . . . Right after they'd moved
there, they discovered that no one was getting any settlements.
. . . You work all summer, fall, and at the end of that year, winter,
after they take all the crops, then you get your money. . . . That's
called a settlement . . . they were not giving Black people settlements. . . . So they got together and raised some money and sent
my grandfather to the nearest city to get a lawyer. . . . He traveled
by night as he was afraid to let them know what was going on,
and they got a lawyer there. . . . They finally took it to court and

got a settlement, which was pretty good at that time. So they started getting money at the end of the year.

Women, as well as men, are remembered with pride in the way they dealt with racism. Says one woman:

> I have fragments of stories . . . the thing that I liked was not like a story, but it's like a combination of things, of strength, of the determination of my grandmother and my great grandmother, of not letting slavery or the way Blacks were perceived in those times destroy them as people. For them to be able to say I am who I am and that I'm strong and I'm proud . . . I appreciate that because I think it was a lot harder for them to do it then than it is for us to do it now.

But sometimes the memories become a source of pain and anger. The shock, anger, and fear experienced by a 13-year-old Black child as he stared at a lifeless body, hanging from a tree, was powerful enough to transcend the span of a generation. It is the stuff of which nightmares are made. Yet, it was reality for one respondent's father. His now grown son still remembers:

> There's one particular story that stands out . . . having to do with racial discrimination when he was growing up as a kid. He said when he was about 13 years old, he saw a man who was lynched by, I guess, Klan. That stands out more than any other story . . . sometimes when I think about it, the bitterness comes out.

The reality of racism was very much a part of the socialization process, as indicated by the stories they described. Even without these stories, the respondents had race-related experiences of their own to educate them. For example, one woman recounts:

> We had a very unfortunate situation. . . . Dad had a very good job at the arsenal during the wartimes and they had explosions. . . . In the area where they had the explosions they'd start taking out all the White people and replacing them with Blacks. So my dad refused to go into that particular area because he wasn't trained for it and he was doing his job quite well. . . . They gave him a choice, either there or out. So he came out.

Another respondent, one of the fathers, describes the first time he realized the significance of race, that there was a distinction made between Whites and Blacks in his community. His childhood dream was to have a pony of his own. The dream did not seem so farfetched, since there was a boy his own age, not far from where he lived, who had a pony. It seemed only reasonable that he might have one too, until his mother explained:

> My mother said, "It's unfortunate that we live in a society . . . where both Dad and I teach and we can't afford it. Ponies are things only the rich may have." She used the term "rich White people."

These personal experiences did not exist as isolated incidents, but were instead placed in a historical context by their extended family members. Perhaps this context, combined with the emotional support of family members and a supportive community network, provided the respondents some protection from the negative psychological impact of racism.

The question that seems to naturally follow is, "Do their children have the same protection?" Or has there been a change in this regard as well? As has already been mentioned, the support of the church is absent for most of them. How involved are these Sun Beach families with their extended families? The initial expectation was that their involvement would be minimal, assuming that the families were too far away from their families of origin for there to be any extensive contact. But in fact, due to a process of chain migration, a pattern that seems common among Black families (Mueller and Ladd, 1970), several of the adults have either a parent or sibling within easy visiting distance, some as close as in the same city, other within a two-/or four-hour drive.

However, there is a difference between physical and psychological proximity. Both factors need to be considered in evaluating the extended family's contemporary sphere of influence. Table 3 indicates the location of the geographically closest parent or sibling as well as the frequency of contact with that relative. It should be noted that some of the respondents have other relatives such as cousins, aunts and uncles, or great aunts and uncles who were as close, and in one or two instances closer, geographically, than a parent or sibling. However, all of the respondents indicate having little or no regular contact with these more genealogically distant relatives, despite the closer physical distance. As might be expected, those 9 participants who have parents or siblings in

Table 3
Factors Related to Extended Family Interaction

	Adults N = 20
Location of closest relative	
In Sun Beach County	9
Elsewhere in California	5
In another state	6
Frequency of contact with closest relative	
Once a week or more	7
Every other week	2
Monthly	0
Few times a year	5
Once a year	5
No regular contact	1

	Families N = 10
Type of assistance received from extended family	Number of families receiving each type
Financial	4
Child care	6
Recreational	6
Educational	4
Religious	6
Emotional	8
Household	3
None indicated	2

the county are among the 9 who have in-person contact with a member of their extended family at least every other week. Of the remaining 11 whose physical contact is much less frequent, 7 mention that they have phone contact ranging in frequency from calls on a weekly basis to a few times a year. All of the adults have at least some contact with members of their families of origin.

In fact, in response to my questions, several of the parents indicate that they have received some form of assistance from extended family members, as shown in Table 3. Husbands and wives do not always agree about the nature of assistance received. For example, one spouse may mention a form of assistance that the other spouse does not include. The family is counted as receiving assistance in a particular area if either spouse indicates that this is the case. In only one case do both spouses agree that no assistance is being received from their respective families. However, based on other information provided by this couple, they do have frequent interaction with extended family members.

Perhaps with the exception of emotional support and, for 3 of the families, child care, the assistance received does not appear to be on a regular or ongoing basis, but is available on an as-needed basis. For example, a couple of the mothers mention the fact that a relative had come to help with child care and housework following respective periods of illness, but they do not receive such assistance regularly.

It seems clear that all of these upwardly mobile adults have been able to maintain supportive relationships with at least some extended family members through their visits and phone calls. To what extent are their children included in this interaction? Although one child has never met his father's relatives, all of the other parents describe their children's relationship to members of either side of the family as either "close" or "very close." Some of those whose closest relatives live outside of Sun Beach County regretfully point out, however, that the relationships are hindered by the distance.

Perhaps another barometer of the psychological connections between the participating families and their extended families can be seen in the parents' responses to the question, "What things do your relatives teach your children?" Despite, in several instances, the obstacle of distance and/or infrequent contact, are the grandparents, aunts, and uncles a socializing force in the lives of the children?

For 2 parents, the answer was "no." Their children see their relatives so infrequently that "there's not really much teaching going on." But, from the point of view of most of the parents, the answer is "yes." The values most often mentioned are the traditional ones of love, respect for elders, and discipline.

Yet several of these parents also express ambivalence about some of the things extended family members teach. For example, one mother describes the confusion that can result when parents and grandparents have different frames of reference.

> I think kids get mixed messages sometimes because we tend to see life just a little bit different than either set of parents, and sometimes like, with our son, we told him at one point not to let anybody call him a "boy" and his grandfather got really upset because our son told him, "Don't call me boy." . . . You can't

please everybody all the time, you know, but I'm sure it's confusing to the kids.

Sometimes what is learned from relatives has to be unlearned at home, as another parent explains:

> I'm thinking about some of the experiences I've had trying to *un*teach my kids some of the things. For example, because we are the only members of our faith in the family . . . I've had to work with them not to reject the beliefs of my relatives, but to . . . understand the differences in the way they believe, and which we believe. . . . We find that usually when they spend a considerable amount of time with relatives, they come home and there is a period of . . . adjustment where we have to take what they've picked up and put it in proper perspective in regard to our . . . philosophy and value system.

Perhaps this ambivalence is a common phenomenon, a natural result of any "generation gap." On the other hand, does it play a role in keeping these families at their distance? The answer is unclear.

Do extended family members play a supportive role in the lives of the children? Perhaps the answer is a qualified "yes." For the three families who received regular child care assistance from their relatives, there is no question that those children have a family network similar to that which their parents experienced. For the others, there is some contact, some closeness, though perhaps not the depth and/or range of the extended family relationships that their parents knew. It is a long way from sitting on a porch some hot Sunday afternoon after church with grandparents, and "loads of aunties, and uncles, and cousins" talking about the old days, to going to the mall with Mom to shop while Dad watches Sunday football. In some families, the distance from one generation's experience to that of the next does not stretch quite this far, but in other families, it does. For these families and their children, what is the result of the change?

One apparent result is that the children simply know less than their parents did in childhood, less about who their relatives are as individuals and as members of a family with a history. While most of the parents are able to talk at length about the family stories they heard as children, their own children are unable to do so. In fact, 6 of the 15 children interviewed say they have never been told any family stories. Of the 9 who indicate that they have heard some, only 3 could give me a rough description of what the stories are about. Unlike the adults, none of the children actually recount a story for me. All but 1 of these 9 children indicate that it is their parents rather than extended family members who most often tell them the stories, a fact which is probably a reflection of the limited contact most of them have with their extended families.

Perhaps related to their lack of knowledge about family stories is the children's generally limited ability to describe extended family members to me. When asked to tell me about their parents' own childhoods or something about their grandparents' lives, past or present, they are apparently unable to recall very much information.

However, since both children who have frequent contact with their relatives as well as those who have infrequent contact give similar kinds of descriptions, the limited information they provide may be due to their discomfort in an unfamiliar interview situation, rather than their lack of knowledge. In the following example, a 12-year-old boy describes his paternal grandparents whom he sees at least twice a month:

> She has a son and she lives with her husband. . . . I think she has three sisters and two brothers, and that's all. . . . Sometimes she cares and sometimes she doesn't. She's nice. . . . My grandfather works a lot in the yard, like putting cement down, he takes care of everything. He's really nice. That's all.

There is very little difference between this description and the description of his maternal grandparents, whom he sees only once a year at best. Another child, a 13-year-old who visits his grandparents several times a year, acknowledges that he really doesn't know very much about his grandparents except that his grandmother "is a great person and can cook good." Although he describes himself as having been "real close" to his grandfather until he died, he says he doesn't know much about him, either.

Perhaps the information they do share, the knowledge of the emotional closeness and that their relatives are "nice" people who "care a lot," is the information which is the most salient for them. One 12-year-old girl describes at length her attachment to her grandmother and now deceased grandfather, who lived several states away.

> Well, I really love my other grandma. I really like her a lot because . . . she's done a lot for us . . . she's really a nice grandmother. She watched after us when there was no one to watch after us because my mom was going to school. . . . I remember like when we used

to take baths, she used to put Vaseline over us and stuff, she took
care of us really good. . . . We lived with her before we came out
here . . . five or six years ago. . . . That was kind of sad to leave
her, but . . . when we get a chance to go and visit her, we go . . .
like we go in December or July. And when we get to see her, we
do a lot of cooking with her. She likes to make biscuits and fudge
. . . she always makes fudge for us before we go back home. . . .
We talk to her every once in a while. . . . They don't have as much
as people do out here, so we call her so we can talk as long as we
would like to instead of her having to pay for talking a real long
time. . . . My grandfather was really nice. I liked him a lot too.
. . . You know, you can tell when you're being loved in a family
. . . I think my grandfather really loved us.

Since this girl obviously had a great deal of early contact with her
grandparents, and later maintained that relationship, despite the
geographical distance between them, one might expect that she would
know a lot about them and their lives. But like the other children, she
does not describe them in terms of their personal history but in terms
of their emotional relationship to her.

It is interesting to note that the children also say very little about their
parents' personal history, a topic with which they might be more
familiar. Especially since, in most cases, their parents' childhood environment was so different from their own, I was curious about the
degree to which the children had been made aware of the struggles of
their parents' childhood. One of these children makes a brief reference
to her father's extreme poverty with the understatement, "He wasn't
exactly what you would call rich." Two children from another family
also refer to their father's childhood, but with different accents on the
struggle involved. One mentions only that his father "liked sports,"
"used to work on a farm," and "would always go to church." The other
child shares more information:

His mother left, and him and his father and two brothers, like
every place where his father goes to work, he had to go with them,
so they'd help him out. They had to pick cotton, all this stuff.

If children in the other 8 families have any of this kind of information
about their own parents, they decline to mention it. Though explanations other than lack of knowledge can be used to account for the
reticence of the children on this subject (the egocentrism of the age

group involved, or the unfamiliar interview situation, for example), it seems safe to conclude that the degree of exposure to their families' oral histories is less than in the generation before.

One mother observes, when recollecting the family stories she heard as a child, that:

> I realize that those stories took in a lot of people . . . I mean cousins, second, first, third, all the way down, grandmothers, that type of thing, and I realize here that's not as widespread. . . . We haven't extended as far out as when I was involved, and I think that a lot of that too was I saw that extension and having so many people to please as a negative in a way. It got in the way of doing or being who you wanted to be. I guess I've kind of cut that off for my kids. I don't know what effect that'll have on them.

This mother sees the change perhaps bringing freedom, and increased opportunity for self-expression, while another mother quoted earlier, sees it bringing isolation for her children.

That there has been some change in the social fabric of family and community relationships for most of these parents is clear. Although they share the values of previous generations, their opportunities for education and economic mobility have led them away from their tightly woven networks of extended family, church, and community members. As a result, their children's growing-up experience is different in significant ways from their own. Whatever value is attached to them, these changes are certainly in part related to the difference between the communities in which their childhoods were spent and the community in which they live now. Perhaps a better understanding of the meaning these changes have for the individual families can be achieved by examining the parents' perceptions of those differences, their perceptions of Sun Beach, and their views of their own positions within it.

4

Troubled in Paradise?

> *"I remember where I grew up and it was the pits. Old country town. Outhouses, the whole shot . . . no lawn. We played outside in the dirt. . . . Sun Beach is a lot prettier . . . "*

What does it mean to be Black in Sun Beach, to live in the place some call "paradise?" Is it the ultimate symbol of success? Are "congratulations" in order? Perhaps. But everything has its cost. Will one pay in isolation, alienation, rootlessness? What price must one pay for a piece of paradise? Is the price too high? It depends. The costs and benefits must be weighed, but each family's scale of measurement is different. The final balance is heavily influenced by one's own frame of reference, the parameters of one's experience. To what can Sun Beach life be compared?

Each respondent was asked to compare Sun Beach to the community in which he or she grew up. The few who lived in Sun Beach as children were asked to compare the Sun Beach they knew then to what it is now. As might be expected, almost all see the communities as very different, though there is variation in their descriptions of the differences. For the man quoted above, the most significant difference is the contrast in living conditions between there and here, then and now. The same is true for another. Laughing at the magnitude of the difference, he says:

> Well, the streets are paved. . . . The one I grew up in was all dirt roads. . . . It was all Black folks in the community, we had a few, very few White people that lived off to the left of us. . . . We used

to work for them because they'd pay us to work. It was all
business. . . . Just the house itself is different. A house that you
don't have to lay down and look up and see the stars at night, you
know. It was bad.

For both of these men, the physical change in their surroundings is
clearly seen as an improvement. But it is not the only change. The
second respondent also mentions the difference in the racial composition of the communities. Though not the most salient difference for him,
it is for some of the others that were interviewed. However, whether
moving from a predominantly Black to a predominantly White community represents an improvement is a debatable issue.

One man, having spent the impressionable years of his adolescence
in Sun Beach, describes his own thinking on the matter. He says:

The fact of the matter is after we got here, after the first couple
of years, I really started enjoying this place. . . . We had the ocean,
we had the mountains, and I mean it was just a nice area. . . . It
was something different about the place. You didn't have a heavy
concentration of Black people so in some respects that was kind
of prideful to me because you'd hear about the ghetto and having
central areas with Black people ripping off each other, but Sun
Beach seemed so conservative and so *nice*. . . . You didn't have
the problems that you had in the little hick town I was raised in.

Discovering how the "other half" lived was an eye-opening experience,
and he liked what he saw. It was true that most of the other half was
White, but not all of them were, and that was an eye-opener, too. It was
nice to be one of those chosen few, one of those Blacks who could make
it through the *front* door of one of those Sun Beach mansions.

I really started to establish good ties with people other than my
own background. I really started getting along with White people,
which I really didn't think I would. People were inviting me here
and there and I was seeing things I'd never seen before. I'd been
invited to a couple of mansions and seeing how the other half
lived, and I really . . . appreciated those things, things that I . . .
wanted in life myself. . . . I just really liked . . . looking at homes
and stuff, and being exposed to not *too* many Black people, but
those ones that I was exposed to were those that were making it.
I really felt good about that, it kind of made me feel special. . . .

> Living a place like here, you really have some advantages where you don't have to compete against your own people . . . we are a commodity, and people here in this area are going to appreciate what we have to offer.

His wife, who lived in a Black middle-class neighborhood until her college years, expresses a different point of view. Having experienced a certain level of comfort in her youth, she is less dazzled by the sparkle of Sun Beach. As she says:

> Sun Beach is quite different . . . the largest place I've lived, you know. . . . There are hardly any Black folks here. Where I came from it was segregated. I didn't even know it was segregation. It was a Black community. I mean, so what? We were all together, it was great. We had role models, we had professional role models. That felt real good, I liked that. You also had people that knew you and your family, and would pass on information that (laughs) you didn't want to get back to your parents.

Implied in her response is a sense of loss, perhaps the loss of a certain cohesiveness within that community that she apparently does not experience now. This idea is also suggested by another mother's response. Greatly expanding on this theme, she explains in detail what she sees being lost in the move from one community to the other:

> I lived in a segregated community and then I came here . . . and I see the advantages of both and the disadvantages of both. For example, the same with education. I see . . . definite advantages of the segregated education compared to the integrated. . . . I feel that there are more disadvantages in integrated education than in segregated. The disadvantages? The lack of caring in the counselors and teachers, the way they shuffle kids into little slots and say, "Well, all Black kids are this, that and the other." The caring isn't the same. In a segregated school, a teacher will recognize the student's potential and even if the student is not . . . an exceptional student . . . the teacher will say to you, "Hey, you're not doing the best that you can do. I know that you can do better," and they'll push that child, and that child will succeed. In an integrated school that child is labeled as lazy, you know, dysfunctional, doesn't have the ability to concentrate . . . in the

segregated school, teachers will take that same child and it will
be a different story. . . . Black teachers want to see Black children
succeed and I don't think that White teachers and educators have
that same desire to see Black kids succeed, and so there is a
definite disadvantage.

The caring of Black teachers in the segregated schools she attended
was just one aspect of a general sense of the community's responsibility
for its children. Disciplining an out-of-place child was the prerogative
of any adult. Respect for the authority of one's elders was a universally
held value, and every child knew the rules. She recalls:

In the community where I grew up, everybody was a part of my
family. . . . Every female in that neighborhood was like my
mother. . . . All the kids in the neighborhood belonged to
everybody, so it was like you had this huge gigantic extended
family and there was nowhere you could go where someone
didn't know you and did not know who you belonged to, and did
not know whether you were out of place, and nobody had any
qualms about saying, "You know you're not supposed to be doing
that," and no child would have even thought about saying, "Well,
hey, you're not my mother, you can't tell me what to do," because
they had every right to tell you what to do.

But in Sun Beach, not all children know these rules. Neither do all
parents. And given the structure of the community, they are not likely
to learn. At least that is the conclusion of this mother. She observes:

I guess part of the problem is the geographic structure. New
people coming here don't even realize that there are Black people
here because we're so spread out, they're all over the city. There
is no Black community, there is no one area where there's more
Black people than others . . . so you miss the advantages of the
extended family. It's not there, so the kids will grow up today
thinking, "Well, hey, where do you get off telling me what to do?
You're not my mother." . . . I mean it could be your best friend's
child . . . and when you go up and tell your friend she'll say,
"Well, that's none of your business." Because after all, not your
child. And so that continuity is lost there that you get when you
live in a Black community. . . . Sun Beach is a very unusual place
to be.

Mothers are not the only ones to comment on this kind of loss. One father expressed his very deep concern about it in this way:

> The community was basically a Black community, for all practical purposes. It certainly was a lot more closely knitted group of people. We felt a lot more relatedness to those people than we have here. We have a situation here that's . . . very, very undesirable, but we're just sort of victims of circumstances. We don't have any Black folks here, not at all. And that's one of the most negative things about living in this area. There is just a lack of Black presence in the community. I'm always concerned about how this is going to affect my children. I don't want my children to grow up not knowing precisely who they are. And one way we have tried to deal with this problem is that we have made it a point to seek out three or four families in the community with Black kids and try to get these kids together from time to time overnight . . . where they will get a decent opportunity to interact with Black folk. And we go to visit relatives often . . . where we have a lot of cousins, cousins who happen to be Black. The community is a problem that's quite different from the one that I grew up in.

Of course, not every parent expresses these misgivings about Sun Beach, but this is certainly the most common pattern of response. In light of the perceived disadvantages, one might ask why these parents stay? Or perhaps, why did they come in the first place? What was there to be gained?

THE LURE OF SUN BEACH

By far, the promise (or sometimes just the hope) of a job was the most common lure to the Sun Beach area. If the 4 wives who came to Sun Beach because of their husband's employment are included in the tally, 13 of the 20 respondents gave the search for employment as their primary reason for coming to Sun Beach. Educational opportunity, too, was a powerful magnet for these upward-bound adults. Some of them came at the urging of a friend or family member who had already settled in the area. In those instances, the desire to maintain the close relationship was often as important as the hope of new opportunities. All the physical beauty of the place was a welcome bonus, but only one person considered the desirability of the area as the primary factor in the decision to move. For one job seeker, the fact that it is a predominantly White community had a particular appeal. Working in a predominantly White setting seemed to represent the ultimate challenge, and perhaps the ultimate success, for a Black man from the South. As he put it:

> As screwed up as America is, when a boy grows up in a Southern town totally segregated, is in a position of responsibility in the South for two years, with a White secretary from Mississippi, is offered a job . . . in California, and you get promoted, America can't be all bad. . . . I've always felt I was good at what I do, was able to compete and do a fairly decent . . . job. I really wanted to see what it would be like to be in a predominantly White situation.

Although employment was the primary factor for most, other factors were often involved in maintaining that decision. For example, one man explains why he chose Sun Beach over another city in which some of his relatives were already living:

> I was looking for a job, and I had friends here too, friends that I grew up with back home. . . . I went to Chicago in the early sixties to visit my older sister. I didn't like the environment, it was too fast. . . . Something is constantly going on, I mean just within the Black community, breaking in your house, stealing, shooting, killing. Not saying that Sun Beach is perfect but that is one of the main reasons. This town is really quiet, conservative. . . . I like that. . . . I like the city and I plan to live here.

Another man stayed on even after the job that had drawn him to Sun Beach ended. Though faced with fading opportunities, Sun Beach was just too beautiful to leave. He said:

> I came here to assume a job that I had the expectation was going to last for some time, which didn't. . . . There was a political battle that went on, and eventually I resigned, went back to school, got my Masters degree, and I've been looking for a job ever since. I'm working now in a job . . . that's not exactly what I was trained to do. In this town to find any kind of work is very difficult. . . . Jobs aren't that plentiful, and the ones that are available don't pay anything. . . . I've been kind of hanging on, trying to make both ends meet. And we like the area, we like the town. It's a beautiful town, it's close to the ocean, it's close to the mountains, it's good

healthy air, there's no smog, but it's a very difficult town to live in. It's very expensive.

Both of these men have been seduced by the quality of life Sun Beach offers, a seduction which seems hard to resist, even by those who feel strongly about the disadvantages. The father who laments the lack of a Black presence for his children observes that he has already been in Sun Beach longer than he anticipated, with no immediate plans for leaving. Despite his concerns for his children, he likes Sun Beach "very much."

One respondent describes how dissatisfied he had been with Sun Beach as a young bachelor. Drawn by an opportunity to go to school, he was dismayed at the lack of nightlife. It was "like a graveyard," nowhere to go, nothing to do, especially for a young Black man from the South. He moved on to a larger city until, transformed by the new role of a parent, he began to see Sun Beach in another light. He realized "that graveyard place . . . was the ideal place to raise kids." As this father discovered, clean air, beautiful scenery, a slow pace, and a relatively low crime rate are particularly appealing when children are part of the picture.

Another parent, a mother who clearly does not like Sun Beach because of its racism, also remains here because of her children. For her, the decision to come to Sun Beach had never been a truly voluntary one. Her husband came here, so she came too. From the beginning, there has been no love lost between herself and the city of Sun Beach. The sparkle it holds for others is clearly tarnished in her eyes.

> What I saw that was so, to me, evident and apparent was the prejudice that exists in this town. It's not as open or . . . overt as it is where you can easily recognize it coming from the South, or the East Coast. . . . It's a very hidden thing, and when you get to know the area, and understand the likes of the people, their attitudes, you can see that it does exist here. Even though you have the intermingling and the mixing of the races, it's still here. Very rampant. It's very rampant . . . if I had had my choice at the time, I wouldn't be here today. It's not a very good place for us, especially for Black adults.

Another one of the women who had a financially comfortable childhood, she is unimpressed with the affluence of the area. It is no

particular honor to belong to the Sun Beach "club," but she greatly
resents feeling as though she is not being allowed to join. She explains:

> Once you . . . find your place here, you still are not really part of
> Sun Beach. . . . Even with getting a piece of the rock, getting your
> house and owning it here . . . it still doesn't make you a Sun
> Beacher. No matter how you want to look at it or what you put in
> your *mind*, you are not a Sun Beacher, and it's because of the
> people's attitudes. It doesn't matter what you own, especially if
> you're Black. It's my feelings, and I'm one of those observing
> type of people. . . . Coming from a background where we weren't
> wealthy, but we lived comfortably, and we always had, to me it's
> no big deal to own a piece of Sun Beach. . . . To me the important
> thing is being accepted and living happily, not having to feel that
> every time you meet someone, it's a surface type of thing. . . . I've
> been here seven years too long.

Yet, from her perspective as a parent, she sees Sun Beach in a more
favorable light. As she says, "It's good for raising my kids." For their
sake, she will endure it a few more years, at least until they have grown
up.

Though this mother's evaluation of Sun Beach is more negative and
is presented more emphatically than those of the other parents, when
considered in conjunction with the already discussed misgivings about
lack of community and continuity, one can not help but wonder if clean
air and a slow pace are enough to make Sun Beach a very good place
for Black children. If, as this mother says, Sun Beach is not a "very good
place . . . especially for Black adults" because of the "rampant" racism,
why does she, like most of the other parents, think it can be a good place
for her Black children?

EDUCATING THE CHILDREN

Given the upwardly mobile character of these families and the strong
emphasis on the importance of education as a means for advancement,
one might guess that the quality of education available in an affluent
community like Sun Beach might be one of the answers to that question.
Although one mother, previously quoted, expressed her view that there
are real disadvantages for Black children in predominantly White
schools, certainly at least one couple indicated that they returned to Sun
Beach after a short-lived move to another community with a larger

population of color because they felt the schools in Sun Beach were superior to those in the other town.

All of the parents were asked how satisfied they were with their children's educational experiences in Sun Beach. Though there is variation in their responses, ranging from very satisfied to not at all satisfied, it is very clear that, because of their concerns about racism within the community, most of these parents can not evaluate their child's academic experience without also considering their child's social experience in any particular school setting, and that both require the parents' careful monitoring.

A friend once said to me, concerning the public schools, "All I ask is that they don't *hurt* my child." Ideally, the school experience will be stimulating educationally, and growth-producing socially, but in a world where ideal conditions are often hard to find, the bottom line may, in fact, be this: "Please don't do any damage—to her intellectual curiosity, to her developing self-esteem. Please don't hurt my child." Probably all parents feel this way, but when your child is Black and operating in a mostly White environment, the words take on a special meaning. Several parents in Sun Beach talk about how they have struggled to protect their children in a potentially hazardous environment.

One parent describes his own frustration when he saw that the school had done some damage to one of his children.

> I became very bitter with the public schools when my baby girl was in, because of some of the changes she went through with unqualified teachers and this type of thing. By the fact that I knew the system, and I knew how to . . . sit down and talk with these counselors . . . I was able to help her get through school, but if I had been the type of parent that didn't care what happened to his kids at school or simply didn't respond to the need of the child at the time, I don't think she would have finished high school.

His daughter's unsatisfying school experience, the result of too many crowded classrooms, and uninterested, "unqualified" teachers, shook this parent's faith in the public schools. He guided his daughter through the system to graduation, but he would not risk another child. He now sends his last school-age child to a private school.

Imagine the dismay of a newly-arrived mother when the school official she has called for information advises her in no uncertain terms to avoid those schools with Black children in them. Assuming this mother, whose child has been in a private Montessori kindergarten, must, of course, be White like himself, he makes no effort to hide his racism. She does not inform him of his error, but instead listens with amazement to what he has to say. She comes away from that phone conversation convinced that this man's school system can only do harm to her children. Such was reality for one mother. She relives the experience as she tells me:

> By the time I hung up, I said this is one of the most racist school settings that I could imagine possible and there was no way on God's green earth I'd have my kids in there. So I refused to send them. I said I'd go hungry first. . . . It was incredible. I couldn't believe it. I hung up the phone and I just sat there and I said I just don't believe it. . . . It was just pure racism. So I said I don't want that kind of problem. And it hasn't been easy. It's a lot of money. . . . There are an awful lot of things we could probably do if they didn't go to private schools. That was when I made that commitment. And I just have not been motivated to do anything else.

To this mother, the public schools of Sun Beach represented a risk to her children's development that she absolutely would not take.

These two families are not alone in their preference for private school settings. Of the 10 families, 4 have had children in private schools at one time or another. All express a great deal of satisfaction with those environments. In the view of at least one tuition-paying parent, his satisfaction is not because the school is perfect, but because he feels he has more power in that setting to exert some influence over the content of his children's learning, and thereby better protect his children from harm. He says:

> I've had many times teachers say to me, "I'm not prejudiced. I don't notice any differences in these kids. I treat them all the same," and my question is, "The same as what?" If you're going to teach them all the same, does that mean you don't recognize that they are Black and that they are different, they have an experience that is rich and that you can use to enrich this classroom? And what we have found in private schools, even though the general emphasis is on the education and inculcation of the value of the dominant society, we have been able to make inroads. I go over there sometimes and tell Black folktales or share with them something about Black culture . . . and with the more in-timate teaching given to the students, there's more opportunity

for their development whereas in the public school classroom, you're just one of the mob, a mob that's very distasteful to the teacher quite often, so to ask a question or to challenge a theory that's been placed before you is a dangerous thing in a public school classroom.

The majority of the families, however, have not taken this route. Instead, they have sought the best public schools they could find, and then watched both the school and their children's performance closely. Like the other parents, they recognize potential hazards in the system. Yet the parents I spoke with found that their own vigilance in monitoring the schools is yielding positive results. One father describes his efforts:

We try to pick the best . . . of the schools that they have in the area. . . . So far they've been to two different schools. . . . We moved them . . . on the advice of teachers who had taken a personal interest. And I feel that they've been doing very well because they make good grades and we do emphasize learning. . . . We feel that, at least I do, as a Black here in Sun Beach, that teachers have a tendency not to be as interested in your learning as they are in their own kind. And I found that once they do see that you are very much interested not only in what your child is learning, but how they're learning, they take more time with the child. . . . We do let them know that this is one of the things that concerns us with our children.

One of the mothers also talks about her attempts to monitor what transpires at school. Like the father who tries to infuse some Black culture into his children's private school curriculum, this mother tries to provide by her presence something the public schools have failed to provide for her children. She explains:

I feel good about their learning experiences, except in one area. My kids have not had a Black teacher. And I would like for them to be exposed to more Black kids naturally, or maybe at least to a professional Black person. . . . Because they have not, I've always volunteered and worked with kids at the school. . . . So I've spent a lot of time there with them, and they enjoy that. Because of that I think it really helped them to do what was expected of them. . . . They knew Mom was on the scene and if anything was out of line, she'd be the first person to find out.

If there is one thing that all these parents make clear, it is that the quality of their children's education is not something Black parents can take for granted, even if the schools are "good."

Whether interacting with public or private schools, for the most part the focus of concern of these respondents has been on the nature of the interaction between their children and their teachers or other school personnel. However, there is another large area of concern, namely, the nature of their children's interactions with the other children, most of whom are White. The painful truth is that no amount of classroom monitoring or talks with the teacher can prevent some child, some day, from attacking your child with that six-letter word, "nigger." Almost every parent has anticipated the pain of that moment when their child comes home, stung by its virulence. Most of the parents had already lived through it. The majority of the parents, regardless of where their children attended school, spontaneously mentioned incidents of racial harassment by other children in the context of discussing their satisfaction with their children's school experience.

Although these incidents seem universally distressing to the parents, as well as the children, there is no universal agreement on how such incidents should be handled. To ignore or retaliate? That seems to be the question. Those parents who addressed themselves to this question are divided pretty evenly between the two options.

For example, one father, perhaps because his oldest child is only 6, has tried to minimize the issue of race and racism. Although "the question of race has been coming up periodically," he admits they have not discussed it. Another father, whose children are a few years older, wants them to ignore racial taunts, but finds a lot of discussion is necessary to help them do that. He explains:

> Our kids have been called names, a lot of name calling. Especially with the youngest one, the only Black in the class. . . . They call her "chocolate," and all that other kind of stuff. The problem is trying to get her to cope with that and to try to ignore people because they've chosen to act that way, calling her "nigger." I said, "Well, you don't have to be Black to be a nigger, just realize that, and when that happens . . . just try and walk away from people and not play with those people because it hurts them more than it's going to hurt you in the long run. When they see you're ignoring them and that it doesn't bother you then you can deal with it." It's hard . . . and she's been doing really well. . . . The Bible and the studying that we do helps her tremendously.

Parents, I'm sure, say a lot of things, and kids have a tendency to repeat things. I'm sure the teachers are aware of it and try to deal with it, but they won't be able to eliminate it. There are going to be people that are calling people names. I just try to deal with it here with them so they can deal with it at school. It's not something that happens every day. It happens once in a while.

Even if a child chooses not to respond when he/she is singled out in this way, can a child *really* ignore such incidents? Does it help a child's developing sense of self-respect to make a response in self-defense? One mother thinks so:

When we were out in Island View . . . they had problems with people calling them this and that, and because they were the minorities there, it was like they internalized that and they had to deal with it. We had to talk to the teacher. . . . Then they went to a different school, in Sun Beach . . . there you have a variety 'cause you have Black, Chicanos, the Chicanos being the largest minority here, and then a mix of Asian students, so the kids were more receptive to dealing with kids of different backgrounds, so they had less problem. People still called them "nigger" and whatever other names, but they were better able to deal with it because they didn't internalize it as much . . . they weren't the only ones. It was like, "Who are you to call me that, well, I'm going to call you this, or I'm going to gang up with so-and-so and we're going to get you." It's more like not taking it as personal, and I appreciated it a lot more than them coming home . . . and saying, "I was called this" (pretends to cry).

Another parent agrees with this approach. Such incidents are just the first of many challenges his children will have to meet in life. From his point of view, they have to learn to stand up for themselves from the very beginning. As he puts it:

Kids have to survive. Generally when you let people know how you are and where you're coming from . . . then generally they'll accept you as that. If you go in tap-dancing and that's even you and I on a job, tap-dancing, telling jokes, tolerating racial jokes and stuff like that, you'd get it all the time. . . . You don't have to use violence, but if you go in and let people know you don't appreciate that, very seldom will they do it around you.

This particular father also makes it clear that he will be there to back his children up if a situation escalates to that level. In at least one instance it did. He recalls:

> A situation evolved last year where there was a fight. And this young man said he just didn't want niggers in his school, that's the way his parents felt. And my little nieces and my daughter kind of destroyed him. . . . And my sister had just spent 88 bucks for a 10-speed bicycle, and he destroyed it. . . . In return, my daughter did the same thing to his bicycle. . . . The principal turns around and his remarks to me is that "Well, they're going to have to face things like that." "Yeah", I said, "but they don't have to tolerate it, and you don't have to support it . . . that's what it's all about." And he said, "Well, the father, we're trying to hold him from coming in here. He's in the next room." I said, "Where's the door? I'll open the door . . . because I'll tell you, the feeling is mutual. . . . That showboating he's doing out there, he can come on in, because just like he's supporting his kid, I'm supporting mine . . . " It was just as simple as that. And when the man came in, he was just like a little lamb. . . . I wasn't trying to be a hero, but they knew I was there, that incident was over, and we didn't talk about it anymore. . . . That was good enough.

Not every parent would have responded this way. Even within the same family, there can be differences of opinion on how the children should meet these challenges. Ultimately, it is the child's decision to make. The moment comes on that playground when someone has said that word once too often. The child considers his options. Dad said to ask him to stop. It hasn't worked. Dad said to "be cool." He's really tried to ignore the taunts, but that has not worked either. Mom said, "If he calls you a nigger again, punch him out, and then talk to him." Maybe Mom has a point. Such was the scenario described by one father. Faced with the situation, the son took his mother's advice. Though initially divided in their opinion, both parents united to support their child's action when the school's headmaster complained. The father recounts this story:

> I talked to the headmaster . . . because he called our son in and reprimanded him for having a fight. And I told him, "Our son was perfectly within his rights, that we had advised him to take matters into his own hands if you guys weren't going to do something

about it. And I want you to talk to the boy's parents and get it straight with them, understanding that they will not allow their boy to call my boy a nigger anymore, or we will take care of it ourselves." And the headmaster understood that, saw our point of view, he agreed with us, he took care of it. We've had no problems from them.

Given the fact that the majority of the parents had volunteered stories about race-related incidents in the schools, it is perhaps surprising that only two of the children made reference to such incidents. One 13-year-old boy had noticed "a lot of people are prejudiced there," but he says, "I don't let it bother me too much." Another child, a girl of 12, elaborates much more on the racial aspect of her school experience.

Well, my school is a pretty nice school. It's pretty nice but . . . some things aren't fair. But it's not always going to be fair, because like if someone calls you a racial name, like nigger or stuff, you know you can call 'em a honky, but they say it's not right to call people names. You're supposed to tell, but like if you try to ignore that person, it's kind of hard . . . it's really hard. Because if people call me that, I'll have the tendency to hit them or call the names back, which you know, our teacher says "You should ignore . . . "

Her struggle for self-control when confronted is apparent, her effort commendable. As she says, "It's really hard."

Imagine sitting in the auditorium of another school, on a field trip with your class to see a play. A boy from the host school is sitting behind you muttering "nigger" over and over, obviously taunting you. A few seats away sits the teacher. You've asked him to stop. He doesn't. She can hear him, too. She sympathizes with you, but says *nothing* to him. As you sit there, struggling for self-control, how can you understand this adult's inaction?

You understand only that life isn't fair. Your struggle continues. So explains this 12-year-old girl as she describes this very incident:

He would just say words to me . . . you know, calling me nigger and stuff, so the teacher was sitting up there just listening to him, so I try to ignore him, but if you're going to keep saying words. . . . You ignore 'em but it's just so much that you can take from one person. And I just kept telling them, you know, "Would you

please shut up?" You know, if you say it loud, the teacher will
know you're getting fed up with that person, because she said it
was getting on her nerves too . . . the only thing about it, I swear
that's not fair. Like if someone calls you nigger or something, they
think you're supposed to take everything, you know . . . but I've
tried. I'm better at ignoring people than I used to be. So that's the
only thing I think that's not pretty fair.

Undoubtedly, she has made an admirable effort, but at 12, the only
Black child in her class, must she struggle alone? Is not the teacher a
natural and potentially powerful ally? Certainly the parents think she
should be. The 2 fathers quoted earlier believe that not only are their
children within their rights to respond physically, but the school has a
responsibility to try to curb the occurrence of such incidents. But as seen
in this young girl's example, the willingness and/or success of the school
personnel in assuming this role is subject to question and probably
varies from school to school, if not teacher to teacher, and though the
parents disagree on how best to deal with these situations, there seems
to be a recognition of the fact that ultimately, there is no way of
preventing them totally. Perhaps it is, as one father sees it, in some ways
a necessary part of their education, given the nature of the society they
will face as adults.

Seen in this light, these incidents and "the teachers that may be a little
bit racist" are not enough to alter the general perception shared by these
parents that somewhere in Sun Beach their children can have access to
a good education. Even parents who have pursued the private school
option concede this point.

And perhaps this is a critical point. The schools are not perfect, their
kids are sometimes subject to racial harassment, but what would it be
like somewhere else? Though there might be more of a Black community, urban desegregation plans might place their children in a
predominantly White school in which the harassment is even worse, or
in less affluent schools, that regardless of racial mixture, are less
well-equipped with the faculty and materials of learning. Even with the
problems encountered, these parents can look at their children's education and see it as one of the *benefits* of life in Sun Beach.

But school is not all there is in a child's life. Having friends, a peer
group, is an important part of a child's socialization experience. Given
the concern expressed by some of the parents earlier about the lack of
a Black presence in the community, how important is it to these parents
that their children have a Black peer group?

IN SEARCH OF FRIENDS

"The tragedy of living here is that they've never been with a peer group, a Black peer group."

Almost all of the parents, 16 out of the 20, indicate that it is important for their children to have Black friends. In fact, the mother quoted above, while pointing out that her kids have 1 or 2 Black friends, really bemoans the fact that there have not been more.

Why is it so important? One mother explains it in the following way:

I'm not opposed to my child interacting with White children or kids of any other race, but I want them to have a Black peer group just for the sense of commonality, and sharing some of the same experiences, and just not losing that identity of themselves . . . I'm not saying that my child has to be around a Black peer group all the time, but at least be exposed . . . at least know.

Another mother, expressing a similar sentiment, pointed out that a Black peer group might help to make up for other elements missing from her children's lives.

It's very important, because of the support. They get a lot if they have a Black peer group. They get a lot of things that I got from my extended family, cousins, grandparents and all that, and that's a socializer. I would say they do have a Black peer group, small, but this friend has kids and that friend has kids, and even though they're not the same age . . . they're still Black and they can play with them. . . . It's a peer group, but not a pure peer group, because it's not people that they go to school with, but it's kind of pushed together.

Offering his own explanation, one of the fathers points out that even though his economic mobility allows him to provide his kids with certain material things, including a nice house in a quiet, mostly White, residential neighborhood, it is still important for his children to understand the reality of being Black.

Sure my kids have a Black peer group, because we make it a point, we have to import them in, or export them out. . . . Most Blacks are doing the best they can, all of us, and I wish I could do better. . . . I believe my children can have just as much as anybody else, but they also have to have reality in their life. They're going to face enough reality just by going to school with these people, but then there's also reality when they're going to have to be able to communicate to their own people and be with their own people. . . . Well, I *know* their best friends are Black, and we're going to keep it that way. And I was just fortunate to be able to give them what they've had. . . . But what I'm saying is that still doesn't have us running away from the truth.

All of these parents are expressing a sense of connection, an identification with other Blacks in other places. Presumably, they want their children to be able to make that kind of connection, too. Even so, the reality is that none of these children have a naturally occurring Black peer group. Neither in school nor in their own neighborhoods do they encounter very many, if any, other Black children. Those children who do have a Black peer group do so as a result of their parents' efforts to construct one, as in the case of the father last quoted. It is interesting, then, to point out that while parents in 8 of the 10 families discuss the importance of such a peer group for their children, only 4 of these families have actively worked to build one. One of the inactive parents indicates that he does not believe the situation can be altered. With resignation in his voice, he says, "You just have to deal with the situation the way it is." Another father, acknowledging his own laissez-faire attitude, explains that he expects his children's friendships to spontaneously change once they get older and come into contact with more of the other Sun Beach Black children at the local high school.

Another couple, however, is not comfortable with leaving a matter of such personal importance to chance. Yet, the demographic reality of their situation limits what they can do, a frustrating fact of life in Sun Beach. Expressing his frustration, the husband says:

I think a Black peer group is very, very important. And one of my biggest disappointments, one of my real concerns is the lack of any kind of permanent Black peer group. It's sort of people that live out of the neighborhood that we interact with from time to time. And they get a chance to associate, but they don't go to school with them. . . . It's really a problem and I'm really concerned about it, the lack of a Black peer group, but what do you do?

What do you do, especially when your son starts to date? I specifically asked this father, who has a son just entering his teens, if concerns about dating affect his views on the importance of a Black peer group. Clearly an issue he has thought about before, he responds to my question without hesitation:

> Oh yes . . . and that's when it becomes really damaging, if you somehow have a kid who fails to understand the reality of living in this kind of community. You can play with these kids, and you can be friends in school, and everybody will be happy and get along fine. But when you start talking about taking this girl out to some ice cream stand or basketball game, then you have the parental prejudices and racism come forward . . . that will create an unfortunate kind of situation, particularly if the kid's not prepared for that sort of racism. . . . We try to let them know that there is very definitely a great deal of racism here, that you've got to be prepared for it. You can't be overwhelmed when you see it. But that is something I am very much concerned about.

His concern is shared by his wife. The only full-time housewife in the group, she assumes the responsibility of doing what she can to translate their concern into meaningful action. If it means driving from one end of Island View to the far end of Sun Beach to collect Black children for a birthday party or other planned event, then that is what she does.

With no centralized Black neighborhoods in which to begin, the very task of finding other Black families with children of the same age and/or sex as your own can be difficult. One family has been looking with only moderate success. They are now going to try another approach, a technique recommended by one of their friends. The father explains:

> One of the things that my friend does with his boys is to send them over to spend the summer with the . . . Boys' Club because they meet very down-to-earth Black kids with all kinds of community skills (chuckling) and let them see what Black kids are like. One of the things that we've done in the past is to send our boys . . . to stay with their cousins in the Black community there, but I think they need to know who the Black kids are in this community as well, and so this is one of the things that we're working on now.

Interestingly enough, another parent also mentioned and endorsed the "Boys' Club" approach, not just so her son will know other Black children, but so he would know some Black children from a different social background than his own.

Most of the kids whatever they may be . . . are street kids. My kids are not. . . . I don't want them to fend for themselves. But I do want them to know what it's like to have to deal with a street kid. That's a whole different thing than dealing with somebody, whether he be another Black child or a White child, who is raised in an environment where the parents care. . . . Dealing with that child who raises himself out in the street is all together different than dealing with a child who is being cared for and so that's very important to me that they have Black peers. I want them to know who they are. They have to know who they are before they'll ever be able to succeed.

"Not losing that identity," not "running away from the truth," knowing "who they are"—clearly the theme emerges. Having a cross-section of Black friends is closely linked in these parents' minds to their children's ability to form a strong, positive sense of racial identification. The mother last quoted elaborates on this point at length. She takes real satisfaction in the fact that her children recognize their Blackness and feel good about it. Especially for her daughter, the recognition came early, sooner than her mother had expected. She recalls:

When she was three, she came home, I guess it must have been the fourth day of school, she said, "Mom, did you know I was the only Black kid in my school?" I mean, I was just shocked. I'm thinking, "Yeah, I know that, but you're not supposed to know that." So then I was very concerned and I didn't really know how to answer her. . . . I was trying to find out for myself did someone at school point out to her that she was the only Black kid there because if that was the case then I was going to deal with that, or was this something she discovered all by herself? . . . I said, "How do you know that? Who told you?" She said, "Nobody told me. I was swinging today in the lower yard and I was going really, really high and I looked up in the upper yard and all I saw there were White folks." Then I knew that nobody told her. . . . This kid recognized that she was Black and everybody else was White, she was three.

This child's sense of herself as Black has influenced her perception of everything else in her environment from Santa Claus to the Easter Bunny. A source of embarrassment for others, perhaps, her mother would not have it any other way. She pridefully shares another anecdote:

The next year she was four, we took her to see Santa Claus, the only Black people in the line, and she goes up there. . . . "What do you want for Christmas?" "Three Black babies." I hadn't heard this, she had not told me. . . . It was the Black babies, I think that threw him. He just turned bright red. . . . She started to get down and Santa Claus said, "Oh wait, your Mommy and Daddy want you to get your picture taken." She said, "I don't want to get no picture taken with you . . . you're not the real Santa Claus." Well, I thought she's pretty smart . . . and he was going to explain how he was Santa's helper. . . . She says, "No, you're not the real Santa Claus and you're not his helper." "Well, why not?" he says. "'Cause the real Santa Claus is Black and you're White." I'd never told her, she'd never asked me what color Santa Claus was, but to her the Easter Bunny is Black, Santa Claus is Black, everybody. So she's tuned in to who she is, what she is, and she's very proud of that. . . . I like that. I think it's important that kids know who they are, and not being ashamed of being Black. It's nothing to be ashamed of.

Certainly most, if not all, of the other parents would agree, and most recognize that having a friend with whom you can identify and share your pride is an important childhood experience. But what about those 4 parents, the husbands and wives from 2 of the sample families, who indicate that a Black peer group is not of particular importance to them? Are they less concerned about their children's racial identification, their sense of pride? Not necessarily.

The mother of one of these families says of her youngest child, the only one still living at home:

He's a good kid and he makes friends easy. . . . I think it's important that he have a combination of friends. He has a lot of Black friends, and a lot of White friends.

This mother seems satisfied with the make-up of her child's peer group, and consequently expresses no particular concern about the issue. Her husband, however, places the experience of this child and his siblings in the context of family philosophy:

If I had to put a summation to my entire family, there were two achievements that . . . have really happened with my children. . . . They know the importance of education and they know the importance of believing in God. . . . Believing in God is not just going to church. It's more or less being able to deal with people in general, with the opposite race, creed or color. And that's so important in this world, other than just being the type of person saying, "Well, I'm Black and everybody else hates me, or I hate everybody else." . . . To give you an illustration of what I'm saying, when my baby girl was growing up . . . I always called her the militant. It was always Black this and Black that, let's get an all-Black band, let's get an all Black team. . . . Well, I guess . . . what changed a lot of that was she ran for president of the school and she was elected. . . . She pretty much depended on the Black students in the school to support her, and this gave her a first look at how Blacks respond to other Blacks in the area of authority, and God, she got so bitter behind that, you know. And I told her . . . that's just a taste of what you're going to be dealing with in the reality of life, but now I tell you, whether it be her or any one of them . . . if they've got a friend coming . . . no telling what they might walk in with. . . . What I'm simply saying is that they don't simply select people because of race anymore and that is one of the things that I tried to teach them when they was growing up, and I was kind of glad to see them, you know, mature to the point where they could deal with that.

For this father, the fact that his children have had a mixed group of friends is a positive reflection on his ability to convey a sense of religious humanism to his children. But it should be pointed out that the other parents, though they want more Black friends for their children, also express humanistic sentiments. For example, the mother who makes it a point to send her child to the Boys' Club, also makes it clear that she does not want her children to be racially biased. In the midst of a "totally segregated, bigoted society" her mother taught her never to dislike a person for the color of their skin, but on the basis of their deeds. Although she didn't understand what her mother meant then (after all, everyone she knew was Black), it makes sense to her now and she is trying to pass the lesson along.

I think now it was just wonderful that my mother was able to teach us in that type of situation and segregation as she did. And so I am trying to teach my kids the same way. You have to like a person for what that person is and not for *who* he is even, or what he has, or what color he is.

However, the couple who have not emphasized the need for a Black peer group not only have humanistic values, but they and their children have always had an active involvement in a predominantly Black church and are among the few sample families with relatives living in Sun Beach. As a result, their children have been exposed to traditional Black socializing agents in ways that most of the other children in the sample have not. Perhaps for this reason as well, these parents have less anxiety about their children's sense of identity.

Another family, however, without church connections or family ties in the area, also expresses little concern about the racial composition of their children's peer group. The reasoning voiced by the father in this family, however, is distinctly different from that expressed by most of the other parents. He says:

> Their contacts are basically non-Black. I think it's more important that they have a socioeconomic group than a racial peer group. In the South, peer groups are regulated by their socioeconomic, middle, upper-middle income. That's basically what it's restricted to here.

For this father, the same one who earlier indicated that he had not discussed the issue of race or racism with his children, it sounds as if class identification is more important than racial identification.

Though no other parent talks about class identification in this way, one mother, who does express concern about the fact her children's friends are almost all White, comments:

> I'm beginning to see this less in race and more in terms of social class, you know, and I think that's a finding of the area. And I would say that most of the people my kids socialize with are from the same type of social class that we are.

Whether this father's attitude is a "finding of the area" or a personal philosophy which he brought with him to the area is not clear. What difference his attitude, or the attitude of any of these parents makes in terms of the development of positive racial identification in the context of this community is an important question which, for now, remains unanswered.

Ultimately, it is a question that only the children can answer. But for the moment, they seem almost oblivious to the issues their parents are raising, or at least, they chose not to discuss them with me. For example, most of the children do not express any dissatisfaction with Sun Beach. In fact, all but one say they like it. The response of this 11-year-old girl is typical:

> I love it. What I like most about Sun Beach is that all my friends are here and, I just like it. It's real fun and stuff.

Of course, unlike their parents, the children have had limited experience with any other environment. Of the 15 children, 9 were born in Sun Beach. The remaining 6 were just school age or younger when they moved there.

Although consequently limited in their ability to make comparisons, the one child who does express dissatisfaction with Sun Beach does so on the basis of its comparison to a place he visits infrequently, his mother's home town. Though his mother describes her home town as a segregated community, this child does not use racial terms to describe either Sun Beach or this Southern town. However, he says:

> I want to live there . . . because it rains down here too much. I have more friends up there. There are a lot of stores and the beaches are really better than ours.

Responding to an inquiry about those friends, he indicates that they live next-door to his grandmother. In response to questioning, he says that he does have some friends in Sun Beach, but he likes his Southern friends better, though he does not explain why. Based on his mother's description of her community of origin, one might assume his Southern friends are Black, while his mother describes most of her son's Sun Beach friends as White. If, at the age of 12, this preadolescent boy, in expressing his desire to live in the South, is communicating his need for a Black peer group, he chooses not to do it overtly by using racial terms to describe his two sets of friends.

Interestingly enough, none of the children ever used racial terms in referring to themselves or anyone else, though their parents had often done so spontaneously. They never referred to themselves or anyone else as "Black" or to anyone else as "White." In fact, only 2 children made any direct reference to racial issues, which in both cases came in response to a question about school. Though the absence of race-related comments is curious, little can be concluded either positively or negatively at this point in the children's development. The fact is that children do not develop an adult understanding of race until early adolescence (Slaughter, 1981), since their emerging sense of identity is subject to change as their experiences with the external world increases. For this reason, it is only the attitudes and values they express in their adulthood that can truly allay their parents' concerns.

Meanwhile, all that parents can be sure of is that, efforts to construct Black peer groups notwithstanding, most of these children's friends in the neighborhood and at school are from a different cultural background than their own. But as one mother pointed out, they are basically from the same social class, so how different is it *really*? Do these parents perceive any significant difference between the way they are raising their children and the way their neighbors are raising theirs?

Only 3 of the 20 parents feel their childrearing practices are basically the same. For example, one mother points out that the parents of her children's friends seem to share her values about education and discipline. Another parent agrees, assuming his family and their families do basically the same things. The third parent who takes this position indicates, however, that the similarity is not coincidental, but the result of his careful parental scrutiny.

> There's no difference, if there was he wouldn't be associating with them too much, 'cause that's always one of the first things that I always scrutinized very closely when my kids was growing up, what type of friends they got, who they're associating with, how their parents raise them . . . because if I'm allowing my child to do one thing, or if I'm telling my kid you can't do one thing, and you're allowing yours to do it, I know sooner or later, mine is going to do that, so therefore that's going to be a problem right there.

Two other parents are not really sure, though they tend to think there is a difference because of a different family structure. They suspect that the children they know from single-parent homes are "looser" than their own children because of less parental supervision. Otherwise, they see little difference.

But for the remaining 15, the answer to whether or not there is a difference is a resounding "yes." Even the father who defined his children's relationships in terms of class rather than race perceives a difference, though perhaps not surprisingly, he sees the difference in economic terms. One neighbor's teenagers have been to Europe 3 or 4 times. Another neighbor spends $13,000 a year to send his son to a private college. This father doesn't have that kind of money and is raising his children to understand that limitation.

The rest, however, describe what they see as basic differences primarily in terms of the degree of permissiveness and/or tolerance of racial differences. In all cases, White parents are considered to be more permissive and less tolerant of racial differences than these parents are themselves. One father elaborates on the latter perception, basing his comments on his children's experiences in the neighborhood.

> Well, my kids came and told me that my neighbor won't let her kids play with my kids. And my little daughter, she don't know anything about being prejudiced . . . so she comes and tells us this. We know what's going on. . . . They are teaching their kids resentment or making them think that they're better than so-and-so's kids and I think that's a difference. I wouldn't do my kid that way. . . . I think in that way some of the White people in our area that have kids are different. Not all of them, but there are some.

Addressing herself to both the issue of racial tolerance and attitudes towards discipline, another parent comments:

> I just think Black families tend to be more strict disciplinarians than Whites, and teach them responsibilities at an earlier age. . . . I don't know how White families raise their children in terms of racial awareness, and who and who not to select as friends. . . . I will not raise my child to believe White people are bad, and not to have White friends. I don't want my child to grow up racist or prejudiced, because I think in time the child will see for themselves, but I don't want to instill my feelings on them.

Although certainly it must be upsetting to have one's child rejected by others on the basis of race, the issue of different standards of discipline may be in some ways more disconcerting. The White child who will not play with a Black one is perhaps not going to be much of a socializing influence because of the limited interaction between the two. However, if the White child is a valued friend, the power to influence is increased. As the father quoted earlier said, "If I'm telling my kid you can't do one thing, and you're allowing yours to do it, I know sooner or later, mine is going to do that, so therefore that's going to be a problem right there."

Several of the parents describe their concern about just this type of situation. For example, one mother notes:

The kids have a totally different outlook on life. They don't respect their parents. I've even seen friends of my daughter's really smart-mouth their parents . . . and so I look at my daughter and say, "Don't you try it."

In families where respect for adults is highly valued, a child who "talks back" quickly earns persona-non-grata status. Any child who forgets that will be swiftly reminded.

For the Black parent in a setting where one's values are challenged rather than reinforced, teaching children to be independent thinkers is an act of self-defense. One mother describes her efforts to do just that:

Some of the neighbors' kids are a lot younger than our children and some of the things I have seen these children do, I would not allow my children to do. Even if I heard of it, they would get disciplined for it. Because I see that the parents don't teach them respect of other people, and especially adults. . . . We try to teach them not to follow other kids to do the bad things that you see them doing, and if you do, you walk away. I see these other kids, they follow . . . whatever the other one does, they do too. So I can see a difference in their raising.

Not all the parents share the perception of difference, but as previously indicated, it seems clear that those who do see it not as something idiosyncratic to them as a family but part of a cultural pattern found among many Black families. It is something they knew as children, and hold on to as important today. One father sums up this prevailing attitude simply:

Well, I think the average Black family, their kids are more disciplined than the average White family's kids would be. I really do feel that . . . this all started over 400 years ago. We were raised that way, from our foreparents, and it was handed down to our parents, as far as to have respect for yourself and respect for your parents, older people, especially your parents.

CULTIVATING BLACKNESS

Listening to the parent's perceptions of the differences, with the awareness that their children are constantly interacting with children and adults from backgrounds different from their own, one wonders if the parents feel at times as though they are perhaps under siege, their children being inculcated with values not of the parents' own choosing. I asked if they were aware of raising their children any differently because of the nature of the community in which they were living.

Seven of the parents said "yes" to this question. Of this group, 3 parents, all of them mothers, talk explicitly of their desire to instill or preserve their children's Blackness. Here in this "mixed community," one worries that her children risk losing their cultural values if they get "overly involved" with Whites in the community. So she advises them accordingly.

Another mother agrees that her childrearing is different because she lives in Sun Beach, but she has trouble pinpointing exactly how it is different. Considering the question aloud, she responds:

> Oh sure, but how am I raising them differently? Well, it's different just because it's not that many Black folks here, you know. Before I think, whether you talk abut Black history or what, you have a history because you see people, you have your role models, old folks especially. They talk about way back when, so you get a sense of that whether you read about it or not. My kids don't have that here. . . . Another thing is like . . . you do Black things, like you know the Black handshake, you know how to dance and all, those types of things that you're around, but my kids don't. They know some of that, but it's not as strong as people when they go back to my hometown.

It seems it is a difference by default. Had they been living in a predominantly Black community, her children might be learning their Black history orally from the old family friends and relatives. They would be learning the latest dance steps from the big kids on the block. But they are not. And she has found no reasonable facsimile to use as a substitute.

That fact worries her, but she has accepted that some of it is beyond her control. With a sigh, she adds:

> I don't know, you want them to be *Black*, you don't want them to lose their roots because of this new environment, but then that's assuming Blackness is a condition of having the stimulus from outside go in. . . . We've been here ten years. . . . My feelings were stronger in the beginning, you know, especially when they started off with the little girlfriend/boyfriend thing and I didn't

know what to do about it, but there's nothing I can do. They have
to make their own choices. I would prefer that they marry Blacks,
but if they make some other choice, then that's their decision.

Yet her concern about her children's racial group identification is
tempered by her belief that even if her children should somehow forget
that they are Black, the White community will not hesitate to remind
them, particularly when they start to date.

The last of these 3 women has a similar vision of the future, of when
her sons are 16 or 17 and are rudely confronted with societal racism,
Sun Beach style.

Here I think that one can be lulled into the belief that there isn't
any racism or something, something as absurd as that, or maybe
they will not understand the essence of racism. . . . That's a better
way of putting it. . . . I think that when a person reaches 16 or 17
that it's a ruder awakening when you face it. And you can't really
identify if you don't, I mean you have all these undercurrents
going on and can't understand what it is unless you have an
understanding of the nature of racism.

It is not a vision she likes, or is willing to accept. Unlike her counterpart,
she feels there is something she can and must do. She explains:

I feel that it's necessary that they get certain experiences and that
none of it will be a natural outgrowth of day-to-day activities. I
have to almost plan out a program. . . . I grew up in a large city
and somehow I have the feeling that that city is typical of urban
Blacks, that there is a similarity to the Black experience in that
city and other American cities. And I wanted my kids to have a
sense of that. . . . My family runs the full gamut from criminal to
college graduate. So I just make sure they are thrown right in there
with the rest of them. And that's been very deliberate. . . . I had
them spend the summer down there a couple of times and go to
summer school down there. . . . I put a lot more effort into plan-
ning to make sure certain experiences take place. I pay a lot more
attention to detail in that regard.

What this last mother makes clear, and to which the other mothers
alluded, is that a sense of "Blackness" is important as a source of
protection from the inevitable onslaught of White racism. If Whites

become rejecting, where will a transplanted Black child turn if there are no roots (or no ability to establish roots) among a potentially supportive and empathetic Black community? Since this theme has been a recurrent one expressed by several other parents in the context of their responses to other questions, it is perhaps surprising that more parents did not express it again here.

Interestingly enough, 13 of the parents indicate they are *not* doing anything differently as a result of being in Sun Beach. Perhaps this seemingly inconsistent response gives a clue as to why they continue to live in Sun Beach. If the previously described behavior of closely monitoring the school and their children's choice of friends is not different than what they would do if they lived elsewhere, what does that say about "elsewhere?" Is Sun Beach really any different than some other community in which they might live in terms of the challenges it presents to these families?

5

Nowhere To Run
—Surviving In Sun Beach

"You know, this town is racist, and if it's racist, move out? Don't do that. Make a stand. You make a stand, because you can't run from it."

Is Sun Beach different? Yes. For some it is better. It offers certain advantages, for both adults and children. Peace and quiet, job opportunities, educational opportunities—all can be advantageous. The experience of living in Sun Beach has altered at least one mother's perspective, for the better, she thinks:

> It's changed my whole value system. . . . I have a lot of middle-class values that I just didn't have before . . . and I have higher expectations of myself and of a child, I think, because it's more challenging. I know there's opportunity here. It's just hard to get it, but to me that's just more challenging. . . . I have never really been in an environment where I had to really look at myself as a Black person in comparison to Whites . . . before there was just predominantly Blacks all around us. And we kept talking about how the White man has this . . . and that, but I had never experienced that, but now I can actually see. I can really see that this is a racist community and how you can get lost in the shuffle if you're not careful. So yeah, I've been exposed to a lot of things, I understand a lot more.

For others, at least Sun Beach is no worse than somewhere else. As one father says:

You know, you have to teach your children the same thing wherever you go. You've got to teach them about the same hardship that you get from one race, and as far as having a lot of respect for themselves and not letting anybody turn them around . . . not to run from it. You know, this town is racist, and if it's racist, move out? Don't do that. Make a stand. You make a stand, because you can't run from it. It just don't work. You got to make a stand.

And stay they do, despite the struggles they describe. As middle-class Blacks, they are by definition survivors. Although, for some families, the hold on their middle-class status is more tenuous than for others, all are "making it" in Sun Beach. Yet evaluating the family's experience in Sun Beach can not be done in isolation. It must be placed in the context of the family's experience in the larger society. What does the "big picture" look like to each of these families?

To assess their views of society in general, each adult was asked, "What is it about this society that makes it *easy* for your family to make it?" This particular question, unlike others I had asked, took everyone by surprise. Occasionally I was asked to repeat the question, the respondents sure that I must have made a mistake. Nothing I had been told so far would indicate that there was anything *easy* about maintaining their status as middle-class Black families in American society, so why was I asking such a strange question? What could possibly make it easier? After their initial expression of surprise, 7 of the parents are able to think of something that makes their lives easier, or maybe just less difficult. For example, one man replies:

I'm not certain we're making it very easily. But I think there is something to be said about this society. In spite of its shortcomings, in spite of its difficult problems, we as Black people have made some progress in the area of education, in the area of economics, and even in the area of health care. So progress has been made, although in some cases very slow. There is sufficient reason for some optimism in terms of being able to make one's life a little better, a little more enjoyable, more productive and healthier, given the proper combination of factors. So I guess it's not all bad.

Others point to their own education as a mediating factor, rather than any helpful characteristic of the society itself.

Given the value orientation of these families, it is not surprising that education would be high on this very short list. But education in and of itself is not enough. As one man points out, it is essential to understand the nature of your own education. Initially put off by the question ("You mean the society of the United States?"), he then offers this comment:

> When you say "easy," I don't really think it's that easy. I think you can cope with any situation once you understand the rules of the game. I think that helps more than anything else. So how well you can maneuver yourself once you know the rules of the game is something else. I think that that's really what's involved, really knowing the rules. Everything that's fed and taught to you in school, that ain't necessarily true. Once you know that, then you're all right.

"Knowing the rules." Another respondent agrees this is important, commenting that, "A lot of people say you don't know the rules of the game, but I think you learn them real quick by watching TV."

One man makes a distinctly positive statement about America, describing it as a "caring society." He feels you can achieve your goals as long as "you know how to approach people." But his is a lone voice in the crowd. Not even his wife agrees with his assessment. She is vehement in expressing her own, opposing, viewpoint:

> *Nothing* about this society makes it easy for my family to make it. I have to stop and think about it hard. I guess the only thing that comes to mind would be affirmative action and quotas. That's about the only thing we've got going for us right now, but it's difficult if you're going to be a Black person in this society, and it doesn't make it easy for you to succeed.

Certainly her answer to this question is among the more typical. In all, 13 of the 20 respondents agree that "nothing" makes it easy.

But with the exception of the man who believes it is a "caring society," they all have a lot to say about what in the larger society makes it *difficult* for their families to make it. No doubt it is the question some of them thought I should have been asking in the first place. For this question, there are no long pauses, no hesitation to respond. The answer is on the tips of their tongues. It is either too much racism or not enough money, or both.

Seven focus primarily on economic difficulties. As one man explains, "If we could resolve our economic problems, other problems probably would fall into place." Not only does money pay the bills, but it opens doors that might otherwise be closed to Black people, as this father observes:

> If we had the dollar, I think we could do a little bit more, I mean this society is based on money. If you got the money, you got the power, and you have the influence. If you don't, you're just going to be another face in the crowd. . . . I'm really beginning to understand the whole power structure within politics, how back-door politics has really taken a toll on excluding minorities and also getting people into these key positions.

For the 12 others who indicate that they have experienced difficulties, racism is clearly identified as the source of the problem. Racism is a fact of life which is hard for these respondents to ignore. There are constant reminders in the environment. For one man, its more virulent forms are frightening. He comments:

> Racism. That exists here. KKK exists here, it's in the paper. . . . The kids hear about it on TV and see it. There's no more Black Panthers, why should there be KKK? These kind of tactics I feel the White man is going to have to eventually get rid of, otherwise it's going to tear them down, or it's going to start another Civil War. Black people are not going to be slaves any more, so what's the use of having the KKK around? KKK, they don't like Mexicans, they don't like Jews, they don't like Blacks, so what good is it going to do to fight all of us? (laughs) You see what I'm saying? That scares me. I'm sure it scares other people in the community, my family, they see this. I'm involved with it every day because I don't know whether the person I deal with on my job is showing racism towards me or whether he's trying to be a friend. . . . I deal with different people every day, some of them are nice, some of them are bad. Hopefully, 90 percent of my business is nice, 10 percent that gives me a problem. . . . But they could strike me the wrong way anytime. I don't know what to expect from them. . . . That's hard.

Feeling the need to be constantly on one's guard takes its toll, but it may be a necessary thing to do. Particularly in times and places where *overt* discrimination is not socially sanctioned, the unsuspecting individual may be undermined by more subtle maneuvers. Some people might call it "watching your back." Whatever you call it, another man agrees that it is a good idea. He explains:

> In some instances, it is pretty hard to label people as discriminatory in that area, but it's there. You know it's there. So what it all gets down to, everybody has their own racial prejudice ... and they've got their own discreet way of handling it without being forced out into the open in some instances. Me, I've been around it, lived around it, worked around it so much I can spot it right away, you know. You can spot a phony anything right away. ... But young people, sometimes it takes them a little time. ... Some person in there ... could have them believing everything is just peaches and cream, and I can sit there five minutes and tell them, "Uh uh. You better watch, because I know better." ... I think that's one of the biggest problems.

Although some people talk about money while others talk about racism, the separation of the two issues is probably an artificial one. Obviously discrimination in employment, for example, will negatively affect one's financial status. Institutional racism leads to depressed wages and a slower rate of career advancement for employees of color. One woman is quite aware of this relationship. She complains:

> What makes it hard is unfairness. Unfairness. ... I *know* there is prejudice and discrimination that exists in our jobs, at least ... in my place of employment, and that is really making it hard for me to make it, and to achieve the things that I feel we should have achieved by now.

Obviously frustrated, she is not alone in her recognition of the economics of racism. It is apparent that the interaction of the two factors places a strain on all members of a family, adults and children alike, as one mother clearly explains:

> The economic structure right now makes it hard because it requires two people working to even think about getting ahead, and when you have both members of the family working, it ... can take away from the nurturing that you should be giving your children. They're getting it somewhere other than themselves and

it may not be the kind of nurturing you want them to have and that can be a hard thing to make up for. You just can't make up for that kind of a lost thing. So the economy plays a tremendous part. The fact that you just happen to have a different color skin makes it very hard to be accepted as an equal person, even to be thought of as a person, to be thought of as intelligent, because . . . society is so used to looking at Black people and deciding all Black people are stupid. . . . Even though there's justice for all, so they say, the double standards are definitely there for Black people. And this affects children as well as adults even in the school system. If a White kid has a problem, you treat it this way. If it's a Black kid, call the cops. That makes it very hard.

But adaptations have been made. At least one woman describes her own experiences with racism, both in and out of Sun Beach, as a process of adaptation. Reflecting on my question, "What makes it difficult . . . ?," she says:

The problem of race has entered a few times, more times than I care to remember really. . . . Right now, there doesn't seem to be that big a problem with me. When I first started working here I was the only Black in my position. . . . It made me feel a little awkward at first, but I've usually been able to pull myself up by the bootstraps. . . . There were discriminations, overt and covert, so I got over that. I figured I'd handle it and I did, so I don't consider it hard anymore.

Not all the residents interviewed have achieved her level of ease with the situation. There is definitely anxiety in the voice of one man, who fears for his family's financial well being. After all, the racial prejudice of one's supervisor could not only prevent advancement but could lead to the loss of the material gains he has struggled so hard to achieve. Describing his situation, he says:

Just being Black makes it hard, because people look at you like you're not as good as they are, like you're a second class citizen, something like that. You got to always look over your shoulder like somebody's always watching you. At my job, I'm the only Black in my department and it seems like they're always watching me, the pressure's always on to perform. You feel like if you miss a day, you might not have a job. So there's that constant awareness on my part, they can snatch what little you have, so that's a constant fear, you know, especially when you've got a family to support. . . . So I'm always aware of what can happen.

It seems that "constant fear" would be a major source of stress. But some might argue that being aware of the threat, understanding your own dilemma, is part of "knowing the rules," and that is supposed to make life easier. Not knowing the rules will definitely make life harder. At least that is the view of another parent, who speaks from her personal experience:

I didn't want the rules. . . . I rebelled against that, and I'm seeing now that if I had looked at it and at least been aware of some of the situations that come into play, I would have been a little more prepared to deal with life which puts us all into categories. . . . So I think if we don't let our kids know this is the type of things you will be confronted with, social class, racism, that type of thing, then it makes it harder for them to live. They come out of the family thinking they're as good as anybody and because of that everybody will accept them in the same way, and that's not true. You have to prepare them. It's important for them to know that they will be confronted with certain things, and they're prepared to handle it. . . . Not that they're any worse off, it's just telling them to be prepared.

Acknowledging that this is the societal context with which picture-perfect Sun Beach must be framed, we can return to the question of "why Sun Beach?" Is there anything about Sun Beach that makes life easier or more difficult? The sample respondents are evenly split on this question, some individuals taking both positions simultaneously. The advantages that were cited before are repeated. It's "pretty," it's "safe," it's "70 degrees year round." Who would not want to live in a very beautiful, warm, clean, secure physical environment?

Similarly, the disadvantages were summarized, still too much discrimination and too few Blacks. Ironically, the very things that most agree make it more difficult are seen by some as also making life easier. One father explains:

I think Sun Beach has allowed us to do better here than any other areas because we haven't really had the heavy problems that I would say some other Blacks are facing in the major cities. I think it's more covert than overt. And I think the fact of the matter is that we just haven't had the radical changes or . . . the type of leader to rally around, to go and change something. I think people in this area more or less kind of appreciate that. . . . We keep our minorities in our place and they seem to be okay. . . . I think because Black people haven't really intimidated White folks around here, I think it's been a plus for my kids, okay, because they don't have to deal with White backlash.

If there is strength in numbers, fewer numbers mean less strength, and less threat, to the White establishment. Also, operating under the rules of the "affirmative action quota" game, fewer Blacks means less competition for limited access opportunities, as another person points out:

If I was in a big city where there were lots of Blacks or where there were a lot of people, the competition would be stiffer. . . . Just from my background I feel that I have gotten as far as I have in such a short time because I'm visible. . . . It can be a positive.

But tokenism is a double-edged sword, and again it cuts. She continues:

There are not a lot of Blacks here. So you tend to get stupid questions, you know, like "How do you get your hair that way?," or you know, people just curious. . . . You don't want to feel like an oddity. . . . People make you feel that way sometimes.

One man suggests that the deceptively pleasant environment of Sun Beach makes it harder to learn those all important "rules."

One of the sad parts about it is that some of the Black people I've known that have grown up here have come away believing that there ain't no such thing as racism, and everything is fine, and they leave here and they go to San Francisco or L.A. and it's culture shock because they don't realize that these things still exist in the world. . . . If they were to stop and look at what's here, they'll find that there's a great deal of racism going on here but it's so well-camouflaged. . . . It's one of the reasons why my own kids, even though they're going to school and getting excellent grades and making lots of plans and so forth, they have to be kept aware of the fact that all White people are not angels, that all Black people are not angels, that they have to be aware of the fact that people are people, and by virtue of their history and their culture and their value systems, and so forth, you're liable to get ripped off by any of them. You've got to keep on your toes. Not that you should distrust everybody but that you should just be aware that it does exist.

Ignorance is not bliss, particularly when it is someone else's ignorance. It was amazing to this man to discover that there are young White people, tomorrow's leaders who actually believe racism does not exist. He continues:

I've seen kids . . . who say there's no such thing as racism, there's no such thing as poverty, that's just a figment of your imagination. In this community, that's very common. I'm always confronted with those individuals who are so naive they don't know what's going on, and it is amazing to them that anyone could come up with all these concoctions about White racism and stuff like that, and "Why don't you want to be called a Negro? Why do you want to call yourself Black? Why do you Black people want to identify with Africa? Why don't you just be an American?"

Not only are they uninformed, but they can have no empathic understanding for his life experiences.

Should he assume the same is true of their parents? Certainly demographics makes the probability that any White Sun Beach resident will have extensive interaction with more than one or two Black residents very low. Add in the factor of White perceptions clouded by perhaps unconscious racism, and it seems like it would be hard for a Black person not to feel like a misperceived oddity sometimes. That so many Whites seem oblivious to their own racism or that of fellow Whites in the community, as pointed out by this last respondent, would seem to add insult to the injury of being so often confronted with it.

One woman describes her own response to this situation:

I just feel like my husband and I work hard and everything that we have, we deserve it, and the community hasn't given us anything. I mean we've got some prejudiced neighbors down the street, I mean real winners, and I just look at them, and turn my head, "Big deal, buddy, I can live any place you can." But I just don't look at it as a problem. I feel if I can afford it, I'll live here, I don't care what they think. . . . I don't understand people like

that . . . Times have changed, you know. . . . We're just able to
adjust where we've moved and we've just had the attitude that
we're as good as you are and that's it. We don't really bother
people.

One wonders what this woman means when she says, "We don't
really bother people." Is her family a self-contained unit from which
members venture out to school and work, having little other interaction
with their environment, or are there other significant relationships or
community involvements outside the boundary of the family? Of
course, this question could be asked not only of this family, but of all
the families in the sample. Thus far, the discussion of these adults'
relationship to the Sun Beach community has been primarily filtered
through the lens of parenthood. They have talked about their involvement with the schools, with their neighbors, even to some extent their
concern about their jobs, in the context of their roles as parents trying
to provide a better life for their children. But are there relationships,
community involvements, for these adults that satisfy their own needs
for friendship and social activity? How do they spend their free time?
What do they do for fun, and with whom? They support their children,
but who supports them?

SUN BEACH SUPPORT NETWORKS

It is clear that there is, for some of these parents, a certain degree of
isolation and alienation. The question is whether or not close friendship
ties have been developed which might offset these feelings of isolation.
Other writers (Nobles, 1976; Aoyagi, 1978) have discussed the important role that fictive kin relationships can play in the support networks
of Black families. Nobles (1976) suggests that these para-kin ties are
particularly helpful in all kinds of stressful situations, including that of
social alienation. Do these adults have "play" relatives who help fill the
void left by geographically distant family and lack of a cohesive Black
community?

When specifically asked if they have any such close relationships
with nonrelatives, all but 2 of the 20 adults indicate that they know or
have known people that they consider as "family." Often these relationships are with individuals with whom they grew up, and who now live
somewhere other than Sun Beach. However, 14 respondents indicate
that they also have such relationships with friends in Sun Beach as well,
often with individuals who befriended them, or whom they befriended,

shortly after coming to Sun Beach. The support provided by such relationships is evident in the descriptions given by 2 of the respondents:

> An older lady here . . . I think she considers me like a daughter. She does *everything* for us . . . like cooking a whole meal, grocery shopping for us. . . . She worked at the same place as my husband and we were looking for someone to do the kids' hair. . . . She said she used to do hair, and she would do it. . . . I was kind of skeptical, and so I just went to visit her. . . . That's how it got started.

> To me, my kids' godmother is my mother, because she's the one that raised me, helped me out. . . . She's a pretty old lady, but I was a co-worker when I first came here. . . . They found out things I needed. I couldn't see well, they got me some glasses. . . . She said, well that was the reason you were behind in your reading, so then they got me in school. I ended up going to junior college for awhile and I started getting good jobs. But when I first came here I couldn't get me a good job. . . . She's the cause of it . . . she's my mother. She still helps me a lot. We talk all the time.

For one man, the para-kin relationship had literally spanned the distance from his Southern hometown to Sun Beach. They were close friends "back home," and he had been a frequent visitor to their house, often sleeping overnight there. When they moved out West, he eventually followed and stayed with them when he first arrived in Sun Beach. With so many years of close interaction, they had really been "like brothers and sisters," his "second family" in Sun Beach.

These relationships are by definition reciprocal. And those who have been befriended extend themselves to befriend others. A woman who had spent her adolescence in Sun Beach describes how her family had reached out to two young women away from their own families. She explains:

> The relationship developed I guess from just spending lots of time with each other, caring for each other. . . . The two of these girls who think of me as sisters, think of all my sisters as their sisters, and my mother as their mother, and they call my dad "Dad." And I guess it's because both of them are away from their family, and it just fills a need to be part of a family, and of course, being that there's so many of us, one more is, you know, just great.

While typically these relationships are with other Blacks, this is not always the case. One woman is amused by the inherent irony of her close friendship with a White couple who were also raised in the South. Their fathers would not have been friends, each of them "very segregation-minded." But, for these adults, at least some things have changed.

The relationships described do seem to supply an important social network for those fortunate enough to have developed them. From babysitting to barbecues, they help to meet each other's needs in the way an extended family would. Of course, those who do not have such intimate relationships are not totally without friends, but the friendships seem to be more superficial in nature, and the families seem more isolated. For example, one woman indicates that while she is friendly with her co-workers, she has "no real close friends" and also describes her family as "a little bit different than other people's families because we tend to stick real close whereas other people don't." Perhaps for this woman, whose extended family lives within easy visiting distance, such friendships are less important.

Another woman, however, who has neither nearby relatives or fictive kin, describes her family as having become "really interdependent and not very much involved with anyone other than ourselves" since they've been in Sun Beach. Echoing the same sentiment, another respondent says, "We spend most of our time with each other rather than with a lot of other people."

There is a lonely tone to some of these statements, a tone which is missing from those who are more actively involved in a support network. Of course, children are connected to these networks, too. It is a valuable object lesson for a child to observe the close "family" relationships that can develop between friends. A useful coping strategy for an adult, it can also be useful for a child. One girl has already made use of such a strategy. The 12-year-old, struggling to endure the name-calling at school, has formed very supportive alliances with other children, including another Black girl at her school. She describes this friendship:

> See, I have a cousin, I mean a friend . . . a lot of people think that, you know, just because you're the same color you're related. So we got this idea, you know that since we were really close, we would pretend like we were sisters. . . . They ask are we sisters. . . . We say, "No, we're just kidding," and then we'll say, "We're cousins." You know, it would be nice if we were related . . . because we're real close and we just like to play.

I asked the other children if they, too, had "play" relatives. Surprisingly, almost half of the children seemed not to even understand the concept. While all of their parents know what it means to have a "play" relative, whether involved in such relationships or not, only 8 of the 15 children seemed to know. These 8 understood what was meant right away, and responded affirmatively that they did have a "play" aunt, or sister, or cousin. The other children were totally confused by the phrase. After such relationships were defined for them, they all indicated that they did not have a relationship like that.

Since in almost all cases, these children are from families in which the parents had indicated that they do not have any fictive kin relationships in Sun Beach, it is not surprising that the children do not have them either. Yet, unlike their parents, the children do not share the notion that such relationships, traditionally a part of Black communities, are possible. To the extent that an understanding of fictive kin ties and their usefulness can be considered adaptive for Black individuals and families, this apparently untransmitted concept seems to represent a cultural loss for these particular children.

Though clearly some families' boundaries are more permeable than others, all the families maintain some formal ties to the community through their participation in community organizations. Not surprisingly, virtually all of these education-minded adults belong to a parent-teacher organization. Several belong to job-related associations as well. As discussed earlier, 4 of the families are active members of a church congregation. Nine of the respondents indicate some involvement with a variety of volunteer organizations.

With the possible exception of the churches, most of these community groups have predominantly White memberships. Sun Beach does have, however, a few civic organizations with predominantly Black memberships. Given their often-stated desire to interact with more Black people, one might expect that participation in these groups would be high among these families. As one man says, "There is a need to associate with Black people, and when the opportunity presents itself, you usually try to do so."

To my surprise, this perspective is not shared by many. A few indicate that they were once involved in one largely Black organization in particular, but lost interest due to conflicts within the organization. This woman's comment typifies what others have to say:

> We were involved in that too, but like I said, it was just so unorganized. To go to a meeting and be arguing, to me, is just not

accomplishing anything, and I just didn't see wasting my time
doing it. So I just got away from that and started staying home.

She has no time to waste. Others have no time at all, or very little.
Certainly time constraints contribute to their limited involvement, not
only in this but other organizations as well. As one man indicates:

I'm so tied up with other things, part-time job, working every day,
back and forth. . . . I'm just fighting for time, so all my activities
revolve around work-related meetings. . . . I imagine I could possibly get involved, but right now, it's kind of tough.

Maintaining at least two jobs and a household, closely monitoring
their children's activities as well as those of the schools, does indeed
seem tough. The fact that most of these adults choose to spend the little
free time they have in family-related activity is quite understandable.
But, particularly for those families that seem to have limited local
sources of support, the fact that they do spend most non-work time
within family boundaries adds to the image of insularity they have
created. Are they lonely? Maybe they are too busy, or tired, to be lonely.

Even so, one wonders if such insularity becomes harmful, particularly in times of crisis. Are there enough resources within family boundaries to handle unusually stressful situations? The families themselves
seem to think so. Though some acknowledged that they had not really
experienced what they would consider to be a crisis situation, most
indicate that they would try to handle such a situation within the
confines of their immediate family first, and then perhaps might turn to
extended family members for help or guidance. However, none indicate
any inclination to make use of formal support systems or organizations
within the community, such as counseling services, for example.

This disinclination seems to stem more from a belief in their own
problem-solving capabilities than lack of appreciation for the usefulness of counseling. When specifically asked about the availability of
various community resources, 14 of the 20 respondents indicate support
for more counseling services. One man thinks such services would be
particularly valuable for someone in a situation like his own, for Blacks
and other people of color "who have not had the experience of living in
a community like this one."

But help could not come from just any source. Not every counselor
would be helpful in a situation like that, or so the respondents believe.
Of the 20 adults, 15 indicate that the race of the counselor would be an

important variable in someone's willingness to seek help, especially in a community like Sun Beach. One explains:

> For example, if a Black person has real serious problems in really just adjusting to this environment, in really adjusting to a White environment, they can go to a counseling experience with a White counselor with a lot of negative reaction. I mean there can be a lot of transference there, you know. They're bringing in a lot of experiences with Whites and they're putting it on this person too. And this person in turn, trying to prove to the person that they're not like that, you know. I think that could be a very damaging relationship.

Another agrees. He makes it clear it is not that he is prejudiced against Whites. He just would want to feel understood. He says:

> Well, it would be very hard for a White counselor, I'd say, to reach into a Black individual's mind, understand what this person is talking about, know exactly where he or she is coming from. I think it would be very hard for a White counselor, especially in Sun Beach to understand, you know. I think it would be of no service to them whatsoever . . . Not that I'm trying to separate the races, but you got to have some of your peers that can identify with what you're talking about, to understand you. Period, to understand you.

As these and the following comments suggest, there is a certain dimension of a Black person's experience which the large majority of these respondents feel would be very difficult for a White person to understand. Like the man who spoke of the naiveness of his White students, unable to understand his desire to be "Black," this majority believes it is a rare White person in this middle-class community who can identify with the mundane, extreme environmental stress of being Black. Certainly as human beings, they share common experiences, but the overlap of commonality is not complete. There is still an important missing element. As one woman believes, a White counselor could not "relate or understand" her hurts.

It appears that whatever hurts these families have experienced, they have chosen to handle them themselves, and it would appear that to them the outcome has been successful. As one man concludes in his remarks at the end of the interview:

All I look for is just positive things, and that's why I'm so
overprotective in my own household, because this is where I see
joy and happiness, because I've dealt with nothing but other
people's problems, negative things. . . . It's hard dealing with
nothing but negative issues and being hated, and being hated even
more because of the color of your skin. It's very difficult, and
dealing with all the negative problems, and then going back and
fighting the administration of the department that you're working
in, and fighting the racism, and squabbling of White males as well
as White females, it's really difficult and one becomes
programmed to be a little bit hard, but then in order to survive,
you've got to control it, and generally I stay pretty much out of
trouble. It's just like playing a game in order to survive.

Surviving is success, not only for this man, but for others as well. Says
another:

I figure at least we do have something here. We got our own place.
My wife's working, I'm working. You know, it's a struggle, but
we're making it. Fear kind of strikes you when you want to pick
up and take off, you don't know what you're going to go to, so at
least I know what I'm dealing with here. And so I figure here's
just as good as any area. You just gotta deal with it, where you
are, you just gotta deal with it. It's just a matter of challenge. I
think I'm up for that.

Although for some the desire to feel understood in one's own community remains largely unfulfilled, perhaps that is a small price to pay
for clean air, safe streets, good schools, and more opportunities for their
children. Surely when it comes to evaluating their lives in Sun Beach,
the bottom line for most, if not all, of these parents is providing a better
life for their children. Materially speaking, there is no question that they
have been able to do that. The question is, "At what cost?" Has there
been something lost in the process, perhaps a sense of family, a sense
of history, that sense of "Blackness," of which some of the parents
speak? And, if so, of what long-term significance will it be in the lives
of their children?

While these families operate without the socializing supports of an
identifiable Black community and, in some cases, without involvement
in a predominantly Black church congregation or frequent contact with
extended family members, they have successfully transmitted to their

children those values which they hold most dear, the meaning and importance of family ties and the need for education. Though perhaps for them "family" includes fewer people and is more narrowly defined than it is for their parents, the children have a strong sense of family loyalty. They understand and accept their parents' emphasis on education.

Yet is this enough? Do the children have what they need for survival? Is, as several parents suggested, a strong sense of Blackness also necessary? Are these children, who never referred to themselves or anyone else in racial terms, developing that sense of Blackness? Living in the context of a predominantly White community, whose values are often perceived as different from their own, have these Black families, with whatever resources they have to draw upon, been able to provide a positive sense of racial identity for their children? Their parents, cautiously optimistic, will have to wait and see.

One mother concludes her interview by saying:

> I guess I feel that the family unit is strong. I hope I didn't sound too idealistic . . . 'cause we have good and bad, but I still think the bottom line is that it's very strong, and I think my kids will be able to deal with society, not without some bruises, but I think they'll have that fiber to deal with society.

Despite those important missing elements in her children's Sun Beach socialization, this woman thinks she and her husband have provided, within the boundaries of their own family, what her children need to be survivors. Each of these 20 parents, in the context of their own situations, hopes that he or she is right.

6

Making Choices

The exploration into the lives of these 10 Black families began with the very broad question, "What does it mean to be a middle-class Black parent, working and raising children in the midst of a predominantly White community?" The data generated by the interviews have begun to address this question. Certainly in terms of these 10 families, a look at their past histories as well as their future aspirations for themselves and their children has contributed to an understanding of their present situations. The discussion of their experiences in Sun Beach can highlight some of the critical issues for families existing in similar social contexts. To label the experiences of these families as representative of all Black suburbanites would be premature at best. But these families do not exist in a vacuum. Sun Beach is only one of the contexts in which they can be considered. They also exist in the context of other research families about whom information has been gathered. To the extent that the information they have shared about themselves can be related to an existing base of knowledge about Black families, our understanding of these 10 Black families (and Black families in general) can be enhanced.

Though each family has its own unique history and characteristics, the families in my sample share major areas of commonality. Primarily from Southern-based families, the parents were socialized as children with values that have been identified as traditional within Black communities (Hill, 1971; Nobles, 1976). Most have at least one parent that emphasized the importance of an education. Religious participation was, for almost all, a requirement of family life. Mutual support and cooperation among family members was expected. As children, most experienced close relationships with extended family members, and respect for others, especially adults, was a norm they all understood.

Now, as adults, they have maintained most of these family traditions. In raising their own children, they have continued to emphasize the importance of work and educational achievement, and the need for respect of self and others, especially adults. As dual-career couples, they have demonstrated the desirability of egalitarian and flexible family roles for smooth family functioning in the context of their own marital relationship. Although most have maintained family religious rituals such as teaching children prayers or saying grace at the dinner table, only 4 of the 10 families have continued to include church attendance as a family practice.

Despite the continuities in family pattern, these families are living in a social context that is different from that of their youth. From families which most described as "working-class," these parents have achieved middle-class status, with higher levels of education and income than their parents had. Though children are highly valued, unlike the previous generation which averaged more than 6 children per household, these households average slightly less than 2. Those children are being raised not in a Black community with few Whites, but in a White community with few Blacks.

Particularly when placed in the context of the issues raised in Chapter 1, these changes in social context seem significant. At the risk of again imposing artificial lines of demarcation on the data, it seems useful to consider these and other findings in terms of the three topic areas discussed in that chapter. What information has been gained that may have a bearing on the questions about extended family ties, social stress and support networks, and the development of a bicultural orientation, which were raised in that earlier discussion?

In terms of the maintenance of extended family ties, it is clear that these families, like those studied by McAdoo (1977), are able to continue supportive relationships with at least some of their extended family members. For 9 of the 20 adults (45 percent) such ties are relatively easy to maintain because they have parents and/or siblings living in the same county. Though most of the parents moved to the area in search of economic and/or educational opportunity, several had been influenced in their decision by "trailblazers," family or friends who had already scouted out the area. For these individuals, kinship ties helped, rather than hindered, their mobility. For the others, even though at greater distance from their families, mobility has not required family cut-offs.

While only 3 of the families regularly receive child care assistance, all of the families except one receive varying forms of extended family support on an as-needed basis. This finding would indicate that, in general, they are still family members in "good standing," eligible to participate in the kin support network despite the fact that they have moved away. When mobility does put great physical distance between family members, adults are able to maintain their already developed relationships through phone calls, letters and visits, though the latter are infrequent. On the other hand, these parents found that distance does hinder the development of their children's relationships with extended family members. These relationships are often described as close, but lacking in the depth or strength they might have with closer proximity and more frequent contact.

The level of maternal employment is high among these families. Nine of the 10 mothers are employed, 8 of them on a full-time basis. When both parents are working outside of the home, while family income is increasing, family energy for child rearing and household maintenance is decreasing. McAdoo (1978) suggests that the shared child rearing and decision making common in many Black families, along with the support of a kinship network, can help alleviate the stress of the drain on family energy. Certainly the central role of fathers, as well as mothers, in the care of their children and the maintenance of the household is apparent among the families interviewed. This pattern reflects the family values these parents learned as children, as well as the family need created by their dual-career status. However, the majority of the families are without immediate access to their extended family network. Particularly for extremely busy parents, the lack of family assistance, especially in the area of child care, is a source of additional stress.

Certainly there are other sources of stress for these families in this particular community. Although some of the parents seem generally pleased with the choice to live in Sun Beach, others express real ambivalence about this decision. The ambivalence, itself a potential source of stress, stems from a recognition that while Sun Beach is a beautiful, quiet, and relatively safe place to raise children, for some of the parents it lacks the community cohesiveness and relatedness of the Black communities in which they grew up. Several of the parents have very positive memories of the closeness of family and friends in their childhood, and perceive this change as a real loss.

In addition, some parents talk about the stress of "hidden racism." Unlike the overt racism they had experienced in the South, the racism in Sun Beach is more likely to be covert, operating behind one's back, and consequently, is more difficult to confront. The undercurrents of racism can be felt on their jobs, in their children's schools, and for a few, among their neighbors.

Of these, the detection of racism in the schools is, perhaps, the most distressing since, in that setting, it is their children who have to bear its brunt most directly. Concerns about institutional racism are expressed by some parents who have observed little or no accurate representation of the contributions of Blacks in the school curriculum, a tendency to neglect the individual needs of Black children in the classroom (i.e., not calling on Black students in class), and the apparent unwillingness of school personnel to intervene in incidents of racial name-calling.

Disillusionment with the public schools in these areas led 4 of the 10 families to place their children in private schools, despite the financial strain created by the tuition payments. Even though similar problems can and do occur in private school settings, the parents who have chosen this option feel they have more power to influence the process because these schools seem more responsive to their input. For these parents, the increased feeling of control, combined with the belief that the quality of education is generally higher than in the public schools, justifies the extra expense.

However, those parents who continue to rely on the public school system for the education of their children are no less concerned about incidents of racial harassment at school. The majority of parents interviewed volunteered anecdotes about race-related incidents which have necessitated their intervention, either in the form of a discussion with their children, a discussion with school personnel, or both.

Reiss and Oliveri's (1983) concept of stress as defined by the community is of interest here, since the family's view and the school's view of these occurrences seem to be a good example of the *lack* of consensual frameworks that provide a common basis for understanding the seriousness of such events. Parents who advise their children to defend their racial dignity, with their fists if necessary, are incensed by the laissez-faire attitude of teachers or principals who seem to think racial name-calling or other race-related hostility is unpreventable and therefore must simply be endured. The stress of having to confront the problem is compounded by the anger at the school's response (or lack of one).

It should be pointed out that some of the parents in this sample are in agreement with those school officials who try to encourage their children to ignore racial taunts. Nevertheless, these parents are equally distressed by these incidents when they occur. Like the others, they feel the need to closely monitor the school's handling of their children.

On the job, some parents feel that they themselves are the objects of scrutiny, closely monitored by the Whites with whom they work. As one man said, "The pressure's always on to perform." The social pressures experienced in corporate settings by "tokens" have been discussed extensively by Kanter (1977). Those who are identified as categorically different from others in the group, and whose numbers are few within the setting, are often treated as symbols of their category rather than as individuals. The only Black amidst a group of Whites is suddenly transformed from an individual with his own strengths and weaknesses to the standard-bearer who is the proverbial credit (or discredit) to his race. While individuals differ in the way they react to their token status, it is a role which breeds ambivalence because of the stress involved. Even if the token is successful on the job, the transformation from an individual to a symbol is a burden. More effort is required to manage social relationships with others who may not see you for who you are, but for what you represent, and the daily effort can take its toll in psychological stress.

Davis and Watson (1982) make the point that for those unfamiliar with working (or living) among Whites, it can be difficult to distinguish normal White behavior (behavior acceptable within a White cultural framework) and White behavior intentionally motivated by racism. One manager they quoted expressed the view that Black people are overly sensitive in their interaction with Whites because they fail to understand the norm of insincerity which characterizes White corporate behavior.

> "You have to look at how White people treat each other," he said, "then you'll feel better about the disrespect and insubordination shown toward you . . . What Black people want to do is have a personal relationship. What White people do is remain outwardly cordial while subtly cutting each other to ribbons, if necessary. We have to learn to work this way." (p.43)

None of the parents in this sample are employed in the corporate world as defined by these authors, but they do operate among those who may have different consensual frameworks about what is appropriate or inappropriate behavior. This in itself can be a source of stress, which can also be compounded by well-understood, unequivocal acts of racial discrimination.

The fathers in these Sun Beach families work very hard, some holding more than one job. Although it would seem that this extra work is to supplement family income, hard work itself may also be a coping mechanism. In capricious environments, where few of the variables can be controlled, it is not unusual to find people who work hard because hard work gives an illusion of control (Davis and Watson, 1982). While not diminishing the need for extra income, this interpretation fits with the ethos of hard work and achievement that exists in these families. For example, while there is respect for learning for learning's sake, hard work and achievement in school are conveyed to their children as necessary strategies for coping with racism.

Although economically and geographically mobile, these Black families are not able to escape the effects of Mundane Extreme Environmental Stress (MEES) which Peters and Massey (1983) discussed. Aware of racism both within and without the Sun Beach community, parents seem particularly concerned about its impact on their children. But MEES and other forms of stress take their toll on adults, too. An examination of the use of social supports in the face of these sources of stress suggests that these families rely almost exclusively on family members, friends, and in some cases, the church, as sources of support.

Historically, Black churches have been an important resource in Black communities for families and their children (Jackson, 1982). Church participation was an integral part of the upbringing of almost all of the adults interviewed, and they freely acknowledged the social as well as spiritual function the church had served in their youth. Yet currently, only 4 of the 10 sets of parents are actively involved in a church congregation in Sun Beach. As Bowles (1983/1984) points out, "The church is a place where one's competency and sense of self are approved thereby serving as another 'refueling station' for its members" (p. 108). Participation in a predominantly Black congregation provides opportunities to recapture that missing sense of connectedness with other Black families who are likely to have a common frame of reference. Undoubtedly, for those 4 families, the church is still an important resource.

Those who have discontinued their religious involvement attribute this change to changes in lifestyle, and general disinterest. Though this shift seems to represent another loss in cultural continuity for the respondents' children, it is consistent with findings reported by McAdoo (1979) and Jackson (1982). McAdoo (1979) found that only half of her sample families said religion is important to them, representing a significant decline from the previous generation. Jackson (1982) suggests that a decline in church attendance by some middle-class Blacks is due in part to their perception that the church is not important in maintaining their social and psychological well-being. She also suggests that there is a developmental cycle of family participation in churches, with lowest participation occurring between the ages of 17 and 40. The median ages of the men and women in my sample are 38 and 34, respectively. It remains to be seen whether patterns of attendance will change as these families age.

Friendships can be another important source of support. Of the 20 adults in this sample, 14 (70 percent) indicate that they have friendships which are close enough to be considered like "family" in Sun Beach. (However, 90 percent had had such relationships in other locations.) Most, but not all, of these relationships had been formed with other Blacks.

Such friendships are very important, particularly in socially alienating situations. A strong peer support group can mitigate the negative effects of tokenism. In fact, if there is enough support outside of the situation, the experience of being a token might actually be a positive one. To go where few have gone before and succeed can be a boost to one's self-esteem. If there is a place to relax, where one can revert back from symbol to individual, then perhaps a potentially stressful situation can become an opportunity for productive growth (Kanter, 1977). For most of the respondents, that place to relax is found among other Blacks. The greater likelihood that another Black person will have a similar perspective and will understand what it is like to be the only Black person on the job, or in the neighborhood, probably fosters the high percentage of close intraracial, rather than interracial relationships.

Although undoubtedly such friendships are important, for all the adults, especially the 30 percent without any fictive kin relationships, the family environment is the primary source of support and rejuvenation in the face of daily stress. Not unlike the middle-class Black families described by Willie (1976), these Sun Beach families have little time for civic activities. Community involvement, typically limited to school and work-related associations, is minimal due to the large amount of family energy already being spent in the generation of family income. Willie (1976) reports a similar finding for the middle-class Black families he describes. Most non-work time is spent at home with the family. Family is seen as a safe haven from external stresses. The comments of 2 respondents from different families are telling examples:

> Being out there in a hostile environment . . . I'm really focusing on the family as being a support, being in a place where you come back, be yourself, and get love at the same time . . .

> All I look for is just positive things, and that's why I'm so
> over-protective in my own household because this is where I see
> joy and happiness . . .

Several parents describe their families as being closely knit and
interdependent, inclined to keep to themselves, or as one woman puts
it, "We don't really bother people." These self descriptions create a
picture of tightened family boundaries. For most, in times of crisis, the
nuclear family itself is the preferred resource, followed by extended
family members. This heavy reliance on the family for support is similar
to that found by McAdoo (1982) and Bowles (1983/1984).

Although 70 percent of these adults generally view counseling as
potentially useful, 75 percent of all the adults believe the race of the
counselor is an important factor, expressing a preference for a counselor
of their own race. One woman's voiced doubt that a non-Black would
be able to identify with her problem or "could relate and understand
(her) hurts" seems to typify the attitudes of those who express this
preference. Again this finding is very similar to that of Bowles
(1983/84). In her sample, 80 percent of the mothers expressed
preference for a Black counselor. Given the general unavailability of
Black counselors in Sun Beach, the voluntary use by these families of
counseling services as an alternative support system seems unlikely.

This exclusive reliance on intimates for support is not surprising when
it is understood that most of these families view their perspective or frame
as different from that of Whites in their environment. As such they are not
unlike the families of Union Park, included by Reiss and Oliveri (1983)
in their discussion of family stress. The Union Park families were
described as responding to environmental uncertainty and unshared community frameworks by withdrawing into themselves and tightening their
boundaries. In many ways it seems like the Black families of Sun Beach
have done the same thing, most reserving their close relationships for
those most likely to share their framework, other Blacks.

Further evidence of unshared frameworks can be seen in the fact that
most of the parents (85 percent) perceive the surrounding White
families' child rearing practices to be different from their own. Differences in discipline and the demand for parental respect are the ones most
often cited by these parents. The degree to which racial tolerance is
encouraged is also mentioned as a difference, with Black children seen
as being taught to be more tolerant than White children.

It could be argued that the family's tight boundaries can be
problematic because it prevents them, as newcomers to the community,

from rapidly acquiring the community framework. But this argument assumes the parents want this to take place, or that such an outcome would be desirable. In actuality, the parents who perceive a difference in child rearing patterns seem to value their own approach. In fact, they desire to have their children exposed to more of the same via the development of a Black peer group.

Of the 10 sets of parents, 8 believe it is important that their children have a group of Black peers. Particularly living in the context of this predominantly White community, they felt contact with other children was necessary for their own children to maintain a sense of "Blackness."

This clearly stated desire to reinforce racial identity stems from what I call a race-conscious family frame. This can be contrasted with the response of one of the parents who believes a Black peer group is *not* particularly important for his children. He comments:

> Their contacts are basically non-Black. I think it's more important
> that they have a socio-economic group than a racial peer group.

Such a statement seems to reflect a class-conscious family frame. Another parent, though she expresses some concern about the fact that almost all of her children's friends are White, suggests that her frame is changing from a race-conscious one to a class-conscious one.

> I'm beginning to see things less in race and more in terms of social
> class, you know, and I think that's a finding of the area. And I
> would say that most of the people my kids socialize with are from
> the same type of social class that we are.

Though this finding is a very tentative one, it seems useful to think of these families existing on a continuum ranging from very race-conscious (to the exclusion of class) to very class-conscious (to the exclusion of race). For example, while 8 of the 10 families express a desire for their children to have a Black peer group, only 4 of the families have taken concrete steps to create one. (None of the children have a naturally existing peer group at school or in the neighborhood.) It would seem that those families who are translating their belief in the importance of a Black peer group into action are more race-conscious than those who are not. The 2 families that I have tentatively labeled as having a class-conscious family frame also have in common the characteristic of being non-church attending, the perception that there is little or no difference between themselves and their White acquaintances in terms of child rearing practices, and a relatively high degree of enthusiasm for life in Sun Beach.

While this finding is limited by the small size of the sample being discussed, it suggests that some Black families may have a class-conscious frame which is more compatible with that of this particular community than a race-conscious one. Whether Black families develop a class-conscious frame as a result of adapting to community frameworks after coming to Sun Beach, perhaps facilitated by more flexible boundaries, or it is a characteristic which family members brought to Sun Beach with them is unclear. The potential parameters of a race-conscious vs. class-conscious family frame, its development within a family, and implications for social interaction and socialization of children are subjects deserving of further investigation.

The suggested notion that some families have a race-conscious versus a class-conscious frame is especially interesting when considered in the context of an ongoing intellectual debate about the relative significance of race versus class position in determining life opportunities for Blacks. In a book which was widely heralded by the popular press, *The Declining Significance of Race* (1978), W. J. Wilson suggests that current economic and political conditions have made class position more significant than race in determining life opportunities for Blacks. Instead of all Blacks suffering under the brunt of "economic racial oppression" as in the past, there is now a situation in which only a part of the Black population, the underclass, is experiencing oppression. And even that oppression, Wilson argues, is no longer racial in nature. He explains that the current economic subordination of the Black poor is the result of limited access to the kind of educational training now required by the economy rather than the result of racial oppression. For those Blacks who have the required training, he claims job discrimination is a limited threat. Presumably, the widening class division between the Black poor and the affluent allows class issues to compete with the issue of race in the way Blacks develop or maintain a sense of group membership.

Perhaps the fact that two of the families seem to have a class-conscious frame rather than a race-conscious one lends support to Wilson's assertion that class issues can in fact compete with race issues. However, the fact that most of the families still define their concerns in terms of race seems to give greater credence to an opposing point of view, represented in Willie's *A New Look at Black Families* (1981). Pointing to statistics such as those discussed here in Chapter 1, he highlights the economic costs of racism for Black families. "When all things were equal, including age, sex, occupation, and other characteristics, Black and other minority males received an annual income that was 15 to 20 percent less than that received by White men. . . . I call this income discrepancy an unfair tax that qualified minorities pay for not being White" (Willie, 1981, p. 36).

Certainly the Sun Beach families are able to control their environments in ways the Black poor can not. For example, those families who are dissatisfied with the public schools are able to pay the tuition to put them in private ones. Similarly, social changes cannot be denied. At an earlier time, restrictive housing codes might have prevented them from ever becoming Sun Beach residents. Nevertheless, the concerns expressed by some parents about their treatment on the job and their children's treatment at school are concerns that stem from racial membership rather than class. Such concerns call into question Wilson's (1978) conclusion that educated and talented Blacks can enjoy the advantages of their class status as fully as their White middle-class counterparts do.

Another area worthy of further discussion and investigation is the effect of this social environment on Black children, particularly in terms of the development of group identity, or what several parents referred to as a sense of "Blackness." The data generated by the child interviews appear, on the surface at least, to provide few answers to this question. Unlike their parents, the children, ranging in age from 6 to 14, generally gave very brief and unelaborated responses to the questions. Their answers reflect little knowledge of family history. Of the 15, 6 said they had never been told family stories. Those who remember being told were still unable to repeat any of them. The descriptions given of family relatives are very concrete, often characterized by the use of such broad adjectives as "nice." Half had no understanding of the concept of "play" relatives, reflecting the fact that they have no personal experience with fictive kin. None of the children used racial categorizations such as "Black" or "White" to describe themselves or others, during the interviews. On the other hand, they clearly seemed to have internalized parental values about the importance of education, family togetherness, and mutual support.

Do these findings suggest some decline in cultural continuity as evidenced by apparently limited knowledge of family history and fictive kin traditions? Does nonuse of racial categorizations suggest deficiencies in the development of racial identity? Not necessarily. Children often have knowledge that is difficult for them to verbalize. The younger the child, the more likely this is to be true. The questions the children were asked, intended to capture their understanding of their social world—the family, school and community—were fairly direct. These direct questions combined with the strangeness of the taped interview situation may have inhibited responsiveness. Although the purpose of the interview was explained, children still may have felt pressure to perform and produce "right" answers to the questions. In the face of uncertainty as to what was wanted, some children may have chosen the relatively safe option of saying little. The style of response evoked by the questions is characteristic of children in this age range. The small sample size makes it difficult to compare the children across ages. Also, at 10 or 11 (the average age of the respondents), these children may not have fully developed their ability to take another person's perspective and conceptualize inner thoughts and feelings to the point of being able to describe a parent or grandparent's childhood experiences in the kind of detail I would have liked.

As discussed earlier, racial identification is influenced by developmental factors and is subject to change over time. The fact that these children did not make racial references may reflect the fact that children do not begin to develop an adult-like concept of race until around age 10, though they observe racial differences prior to that (Slaughter, 1981). Since the community is almost all White, older children may have assumed it was unnecessary to identify other people as "White," and since I certainly knew they were Black, such self-reference also was not needed.

The one child who did discuss racial issues at length may have been inclined to do so because of the salience of her school experiences with racial name-calling. However, this child was also one of the children who was able to provide the most information about her family. The fact that she was 12 at the time of the interview places her at the higher end of the sample, developmentally. However, she is also different from most of the other children interviewed in that she spent her preschool years in a Southern Black community and returns there every year for an extended visit. Which, if any, of these factors contributed to her somewhat greater ability to respond to the questions asked is very difficult to determine, and underscores the need for further investigation with a much larger sample.

Given the possibilities for error in interpretation, it is difficult to draw any conclusions. However, if for the moment, we assumed that there is some validity to the interpretation that the children have less of a traditionally Black cultural orientation and weaker ethnic group identification than their parents do, how could such a finding be explained?

As discussed in Chapter 1, Barnes (1980) and others have emphasized the role of the social environment in mediating negative messages from mainstream White society about Blacks, and in helping Black children to foster positive attitudes about their group. Part of the community structure that has facilitated this process is the traditionally Black church and the extended family networks. It has been pointed out that the majority of the children in this sample are not members of a Black congregation and have limited extended family contacts. Most also have limited contacts with other Black children, either at home or at school. Even though most parents seem to value their cultural heritage and family orientation, their input may be outweighed by a competing community frame, making children more susceptible to influences of the larger society. What might be the long-range implications of such a development?

The case of upwardly mobile Japanese-American families might be instructive here. Studies of upwardly mobile Japanese-American families over three generations have shown that considerable acculturation has taken place (Connor, 1974; Levine and Montero, 1973; Tinker, 1982).

The vast majority of the first-generation immigrants (Issei) came to the United States seeking economic opportunities, with the intent of returning with their wealth to Japan. Given their intent not to remain in America permanently, this generation held onto their Japanese lifestyle. The fact that they and their offspring (the Nisei generation) lived in largely self-sufficient Japanese communities on the West coast made retention of Japanese traditions even more likely.

The Issei sought to inculcate traditional family values in their offspring, and these were reinforced outside of the family boundaries as well. Many Nisei attended Japanese language schools and continued to reside in Japanese communities. The Nisei generation (average age is now about 55) reportedly view themselves as truly bicultural, combining the best of Japanese and American cultures (Connor, 1974).

However, Levine and Montero (1973) suggest that the Nisei generation can be divided roughly along occupational lines into two groups, those who hold white-collar jobs and those who do not. The white-collar Nisei are described as less traditional and more assimilationist in their orientation than the other group in a number of ways. The white-collar group is more likely to live in predominantly White neighborhoods, and is less likely to object to interracial marriages of their children. They are also less likely to belong to any Japanese-American organizations, or to be able to speak or read Japanese. Finally, they are much less likely to practice Buddhism.

The thrust toward assimilation has gained momentum in the next generation (Sansei), the second generation born in the United States. Perceived by both the Issei and Nisei generation as very acculturated, the Sansei generation (now in their 30s) are even less likely to speak Japanese, less likely to be involved in Japanese-American organizations, more likely to have Whites as their closest friends, and have a much higher rate of intermarriage (Tinker, 1982). Using figures from one California county, Tinker reports that the intermarriage rate of the Nisei generation was 17 percent, but for the Sansei generation the rate is now 58 percent.

Despite these outward signs of assimilation into White American society, Connor (1974, p.164) indicates that the view that the Sansei have been "completely Americanized" is in error. When compared with Caucasians on personal preference scales, the Sansei still reflect a number of "Japanese characteristics." He reports the Sansei to be significantly more deferent, more self-effacing, less dominant, more affiliative, less aggressive, and having a greater need for succoring and order than do Whites. While Sansei scored lower than Issei or Nisei on items related to particular family values, they consistently scored higher than the Whites in the sample. Connor (1974, p. 164) concludes that "while the emphasis on the family and the inculcation of dependency needs in the third generation are considerably attenuated in comparison with first and second generations, the emphasis still remains greater than that found in caucasian Americans."

Since there are differences in both culture and the societal perception of African-Americans and Japanese-Americans (Sue and Kitano, 1973), caution must be used in making cross-cultural comparisons. However, some interesting parallels do exist. Like Japanese-Americans, African-Americans can be visibly identified as different in the context of a Caucasian community. Like white-collar Nisei, the Blacks in this sample live in a predominantly White community, the majority of them are not active in African-American organizations, and they have not maintained traditional religious practices. The majority of children have Whites as their close friends.

The point of most interest is that Nisei, who had themselves been inculcated with traditional values (as have these Black parents), were not able to forestall the greater assimilation of their children once outside the context of a Japanese community. Even though anti-Japanese feeling exists and was quite high in the not-so-distant past, particularly in California, societal discrimination did not prevent the assimilation of Sansei children raised in White communities.

Though Connors' (1974) point about the retention of personal characteristics which are associated with the Japanese ethnic group may be well
taken, he seems to refer to personal identity rather than group identity. It
is the maintenance of *group* identity as well as personal identity that seems
to concern most of the Black parents in this sample. Yet the process of
assimilation would seem to diffuse one's sense of group identity.

As Jackson, McCullough, and Gurin (1981) point out, group identification is usually not an all-or-nothing proposition, but is a complicated
mixture of positive and negative feelings. They write (p.256): "The critical
issue is how the individual balances the negative and positive images of
and feelings toward the group, and the extent to which the individual
connects the self to the positive rather than to the negative group images."

As Black assimilation increases, does the balance between negative
and positive images and feelings toward the group tip toward a greater
degree of negative evaluation of the group (to the degree that it is seen
as different from the increasingly valued dominant group)? If so, what
is the consequence? If, as suggested in Chapter 1, personal self-
evaluation can be quite distinct from group evaluation, of what significance is positive group identification (or lack of it) anyway?

When we recognize that group identification is essentially a precur-
sor to the political socialization of Black people, the answer to the
question is apparent. The significance for the group is potentially great.
Certainly the political progress of the group is hindered if those with
leadership potential, at least in terms of educational attainment and
some economic clout, no longer make a connection between their own
advancement and that of their group.

At the individual level, what is the significance of defining oneself
as an "exception?" A Black corporate manager, quoted by Davis and
Watson (1982), described some co-workers who represented a possible
adult outcome of Black children who see themselves as exceptions.

> They've been educated from kindergarten with White kids and
> so there's not a great deal of difference between them and the
> White guy, the corporation will find a place for them. Most of
> them don't know and don't care much about Black culture or any
> other kind of culture. They won't even speak to you in the hallway
> when they see you, but they'll speak to the White guy, and so they
> do have a negative racial consciousness. (p.51)

Known in the vernacular as "oreos," Black on the outside, White on the
inside, this is what those parents who want to maintain their children's

Blackness are trying to prevent. They don't want their children to
become "oreos."

Though the example of Japanese-American acculturation suggests that
reduction in group identification and cultural continuity is a possible
outcome of residence in predominantly White communities, is it an
inevitably unpreventable one? To answer this question adequately, the role
of the family's value orientation must be explored further. A child's
experience of himself and the world around him is tempered by parental
values and attitudes. Parental views of their own group membership will
surely impact on the development of such attitudes in their children. One
might expect, then, that the more race-conscious the family frame is, the
more likely it is that the child will be able to maintain a solid positive
group identification. In such families, the meaning of being Black from
both the perspective of being an American minority and the historical
cultural ties to Africa may be presented to the child as a source of pride.
An environment can be created which reinforces, rather than undermines,
the child's sense of belonging to the larger community of African-
Americans. Conversely, the less race-conscious the family frame, the less
likely the child will maintain such identification.

While more information is needed to confirm or disconfirm this
hypothesis, the issues outlined here emphasize the great need for
longitudinal studies of Black families to investigate the long-term
impact of family ideology and socialization patterns. What is or will be
the adult adjustment level of more assimilated Black adults? Will they,
like the Sansei, retain some core personal characteristics communicated
from parent to child early in the socialization process? Presumably still
vulnerable to the effects of MEES, will they use the same traditional
coping patterns used by their parents?

Although a challenging task, it seems possible for race-conscious
parents to do what is necessary to reinforce a positive group identity
without the environmental buffer of a Black community. While identifying exactly what *is* necessary is yet to be done, one would expect
that increased association with other Blacks in settings like the church,
for example, would help. Parental initiative in providing cultural role
models, sharing family stories, and openly discussing and providing
multicultural experiences could help to counteract the losses associated
with life in a predominantly White community.

The choice of where to live is a very specific one, but I believe it is
symbolic of a larger issue that affects all Black parents, regardless of
where they live. Wade Nobles, a noted Black social scientist, wrote
eloquently about this underlying issue.

For us, we contend, the change from "Black" to "White" is too costly. It amounts to the sacrifice of our children's humaneness. For "ebony" to become "ivory," we and our children must give up the sense of struggle, the sense of righteousness, the sense of commitment and the sense of "we-ness." We must become individually self-centered and concerned with only our personal well-being and development. This, we, in all honesty, recognize to be happening right now. The intensive contact with White people, primarily through the electronic media, is taking its toll and the issue of "people survival" is rapidly waning in the wake of "I've got to do my own thing." In so doing, the Black family is or will give up its "humanism" for a new "individualism."

We, Black social scientists particularly, but Black people in general, therefore, have a choice and the choice is to consciously begin to reinforce the historical sense of Blackness and humanism in our people, through the integrity of our families, *or* allow the effects of Americanization (via schools, the media, etc.) to convince us that our "ebony is White." To allow for the latter is to participate in the destruction of our own families. To choose the former is to struggle for the survival of our humaneness. The choice, indeed, is ours. (p.171)

Although they may not all conceive of their existence in Sun Beach in these terms, I believe these families are on the cutting edge of this choice. Does this mean those who wish to retain their children's sense of struggle and commitment to their group should pack their bags? Not necessarily.

Listen to the voices of two young women, both products of predominantly White communities on the East Coast, far from Sun Beach. Both students of mine, they shared with me some of their childhood experiences in those communities. Their parents faced choices, as do the parents of Sun Beach. Like most young adults, these young women have been evaluating their parents' decisions. One recalls:

I have had to deal with racism all of my life and I never even realized it. I've been in predominantly White schools and churches all of my life, and there have been a number of instances that I can recall when, for example, Mary would get the lead in the school play because she was White and if a Black girl like myself would have gotten the part, it just wouldn't look right coming from a White school. When it came time for cheerleading tryouts, only *one* Black would be chosen as a token so it couldn't be said that they discriminated against minorities. When I used to go to school dances, I never got asked to dance and I never really had a good time because I was Black and I never really understood. I used to get angry at my mom because I didn't know why she was sending me to school with these people that didn't accept me. But now I realize that all she wanted was for me to have some of the nicer things that White people had. . . . Throughout junior high school and high school, I've experienced a tremendous amount of resentment and distrust from other Blacks . . . they used to call me "White girl" and say that I thought I was better than everyone else. When I was around 15 or so, I stopped letting it get to me. Because I don't have a problem with my identity or who I am, and I don't think I'm better than anyone else. My mother didn't raise me that way. She raised me in a predominantly White environment to increase my opportunities.

This woman struggled in her childhood and now offers some advice for parents:

I think that teaching a young child about racism would be very helpful. I also feel that it's important that this happens at a young age because if it's not, it's possible that there can be emotional scars for the rest of their lives if they were to find out from somewhere else in an unpleasant way, as it happened to me.

In another community, another young woman was growing up, confronted with similar issues. She learned about racism "somewhere else" and it hurt. She recalls:

I discovered that being Black made a difference . . . when I was very young, in the third grade or so. All of my childhood friends were White middle-class kids. I attended a predominantly White school before busing came into effect, therefore I didn't interact with many, if any, Black children. I can remember one of my friends saying that a lot of niggers were moving into the neighborhood. I went home and talked to my mother and older sister . . . and asked them what a nigger was. My mother told me that White people called Blacks niggers back in the old days, and that it was a bad word and that I shouldn't condone name-calling like that. . . . At about this same time I found out that many Blacks were poor. I asked my mother why there weren't many Blacks in our neighborhood and why many Blacks lived in one area of the city. She then told me that she had worked hard all her life to give us a nice house, car, nice clothes, money to have treats, etc. She said that those other Black people hadn't worked as hard as she had to overcome the many barriers and boundaries that other Black people were confined to. She emphasized how lucky we were.

At that time I didn't really care that I was Black, maybe just because I didn't fully understand race or racism. I must have been in my teens when I wanted to be seen as an individual, not seen as an entire race. I only wanted to be accepted by my friends, have a boyfriend, etc. Because all my friends were White, I was the only one without a boyfriend because the boys were too afraid to have a Black girlfriend. At this point, I found myself wanting to be White more than anything else. I would do almost anything to impress my White counterparts and to prove to them that I was the same as they.When I was in the eighth grade, I wanted more than anything to date my best friend's brother. We were pretty good friends and he liked me too, but he didn't want me to be his girlfriend because all of his friends had the so-called beautiful girls with blonde hair and his friends and himself couldn't accept me.

At this time, I also found myself hating me as a Black individual and also my culture. . . . I feel that I wouldn't have undergone such severe identity problems if my mother had encouraged Blackness in our house. I think my mother just wanted to evade the whole issue of race and racism. She put and kept us in all-White schools and neighborhoods. Even after busing, she didn't encourage us to interact with our own people.

Growing up in what sounds like a class-conscious family, now a parent herself, this young woman is definitely choosing to be race-conscious in her interactions with her own children. She asserts:

As a person socialized White, I had many pressures that most Blacks do not experience. Not only was I rejected by my so-called White friends, but also by my Black counterparts. At a certain age I wasn't accepted . . . because I wasn't White. Then I wasn't accepted by most Blacks because "I acted like a White girl." This makes me angry when I think of childhood and adolescent years not accepted and rejected at the same time. I feel that this caused emotional strain and added to the identity problems. . . . Society wants you to become as White as possible because "White is right." Americans think you are better if you have less of your own culture and more of theirs. . . . I don't think we as Black individuals should raise our children in the manner that many socialized Whites do. Children should not look down on their race, or their ethnic background. They should be proud that they are Black even if they do live in a predominantly White neighborhood. Their culture and other non-White cultures should be brought to their attention in a positive manner, not through the White man's eyes. . . . I feel that this should be of major concern to parents, especially Black and other non-White parents. Just as we teach our children the moral and ethical system of the U.S., this should be included in great detail.

Although there is pain in the words of these young women, there may also be valuable wisdom borne from their experiences as first-generation "immigrants" to their mostly White communities. They seem to agree with the Sun Beach father who says:

You know, you have to teach your children the same thing wherever you go. You have to teach them about the hardship that you get from one race, and as far as having a lot of respect for themselves and not letting anybody turn them around. . . . And not to run from it. It just don't work. You got to make a stand.

Families willing to make a race-conscious stand may be able to reap the benefits of the opportunities which drew them to this community in the first place, without sacrificing their children's Blackness in the process.

Bibliography

Allen, W. R. (1978). The search for applicable theories of black family life. *Journal of Marriage and the Family* 40(February): 117–29.

Allen, W. R. (1981). Moms, dads, and boys: Race and sex differences in the socialization of male children. In L. Gary (Ed.) *Black men.* Beverly Hills: Sage Publications, pp. 99–114.

Anderson, K., and Allen, W.R. (1982). Correlates of extended household structure. In G. McWorter (Ed.) *Studies of black children and their families.* Proceedings of the 6th Annual Conference of The National Council for Black Studies, March 17–20, 1982. Urbana: University of Illinois Afro-American Studies and Research Program, pp. 1–21.

Aoyagi, K. (1978). Kinship and friendship in black Los Angeles: A study of migrants from Texas. In D.B. Shimkin, E. M. Shimkin. and D.A. Frate (Eds.) *The extended family in black societies.* Chicago: Aldine, pp. 271–353.

Aschenbrenner, J. (1975). *Lifelines: Black families in Chicago.* Chicago: Holt, Rinehart and Winston.

Aschenbrenner, J. (1978). Continuities and variations in black family structure. In D. B. Shimkin, E.M. Shimkin, and D.A. Frate (Eds.) *The extended family in black societies.* Chicago: Aldine, pp. 181–200.

Barnes, E. (1980). The black community as the source of positive self-concept for black children: A theoretical perspective. In R. Jones (Ed.) *Black psychology.* 2d ed. New York: Harper and Row, pp. 106–30.

Bermann, E. (1973). *Scapegoat.* Ann Arbor: University of Michigan.

Billingsley, A. (1968). *Black families in white America.* Englewood Cliffs, NJ: Prentice-Hall.

Billingsley, A. (1973). In J.A. Ladner (Ed.) *The death of white sociology.* New York: Random House, pp. 431–50.

Bowles, D. D. (1984). The impact of ethnicity on African-American mothering during the separation-individuation phase of development. Ed.D.diss., University of Massachusetts, 1983. *Dissertation Abstracts International* 44, p. 3162–A.

Cazenave, N. (1979). Middle-income black fathers: An analysis of the provider role. *Family Coordinator* 28(October): 583–93.

Connor, J. (1974). Acculturation and family continuities in three generations of Japanese Americans. *Journal of Marriage and the Family* 36(February): 159–65.

Cross, W. E. (1978). Black family and black identity: A literature review. *Western Journal of Black Studies* 2(Summer): 111–24.

Davis, G., and Watson, G. (1982). *Black life in corporate America: Swimming in the mainstream.* Garden City, NY: Anchor Press.

Engram, E. (1982). *Science, myth, reality: The black family in one-half century of research.* Westport, CT: Greenwood Press.

Frazier, E. F. (1939). *The Negro family in the United States.* Chicago: University of Chicago Press.

Frazier, E. F. (1957). *Black bourgeoisie: The rise of a new middle-class in the United States.* Glencoe, IL: Free Press.

Glick, P. (1981). A demographic picture of black families. In H. P. McAdoo (Ed.) *Black families.* Beverly Hills: Sage Publications, pp. 106–26.

Gutman, H. G. (1976). *The black family in slavery and freedom, 1750–1925.* New York: Pantheon.

Hale, J. (1980). The black woman and child rearing. In L. Rodgers-Rose (Ed.) *The black woman.* Beverly Hills: Sage Publications, pp. 79–87.

Hannerz, U. (1975). *Soulside: Inquiries into ghetto culture and community.* New York: Columbia University Press.

Hays, W. C., and Mindel, C. H. (1973). Extended kinship relationships in black and white families. *Journal of Marriage and the Family* 35(February): 51–57.

Henry, J. (1965) *Pathways to madness.* New York: Random House.

Hess, R. D., and Handel, G. (1959). *Family worlds.* Chicago: University of Chicago Press.

Hill, R. (1963). Social stresses on the family. In M. B. Sussman (Ed.) *Sourcebook on marriage and the family*. Boston: Houghton-Mifflin, pp. 303–14.

Hill, R. (1971). *The strengths of black families*. New York: Emerson Hall.

Hines, P. M., and Boyd-Franklin, N. (1982). Black families. In M. McGoldrick, J. K. Pearce, and J. Giordano (Eds.) *Ethnicity and family therapy*. New York: Guilford Press, pp. 84–107.

Jackson, F. M. (1982) Black families, children and their churches. In G. McWorter (Ed.) *Studies on black children and their families*. Proceedings of the 6th Annual Conference of The National Council for Black Studies, March 17–20. Urbana: University of Illinois Afro-American Studies and Research Program, pp. F1–14.

Jackson, J., McCullough, W., & Gurin, G. (1981). Group identity development within black families. In H. P. McAdoo (Ed.) *Black families*. Beverly Hills: Sage Publications.

Kanter, R. M. (1977). *Men and women of the corporation*. New York: Basic Books.

Klein, D. M. (1983). Family problem solving and family stress. *Marriage and Family Review* 6(Spring): 85–112.

Landry, L. B. (1980). The social and economic adequacy of the black middle class. In J. R. Washington, Jr. (Ed,) *Dilemmas of the new black middle class*. University of Pennsylvania Afro-American Studies Symposium Proceedings.

Landry, L. B., and Jendrek, M. (1978). The employment of wives in middle-class black families. *Journal of Marriage and the Family* 40(November): 787–98.

Levine, G., and Montero, D. (1973). Socioeconomic mobility among three generations of Japanese Americans. *Journal of Social Issues* 29(Summer): 33–48.

Lewis, D. K. (1982). The black family: Socialization and sex roles *Phylon* 36(Fall): 221–237.

Malson, M. (1982) The social-support systems of black families. *Marriage and Family Review* 5(Winter): 37–57.

Martin, E. P., and Martin, J. M. (1978). *The black extended family*. Chicago: University of Chicago Press.

Mbiti, J. S. (1970). *African religions and philosophies*. New York: Anchor Press.

McAdoo, H. P. (1977). *Impact of extended family variables upon the upward mobility of black families.* Contract No. 90-c-631(1). Washington: Office of Child Development.

McAdoo, H. P. (1978). Factors related to stability in upwardly mobile black families. *Journal of Marriage and the Family* 40(November): 761–76.

McAdoo, H. P. (1979) Black kinship. *Psychology Today* (May), pp. 67, 69–70, 79, 110.

McAdoo, H. P. (1982). Stress-absorbing systems in black families. *Family Relations* 31(October): 479–88.

McCubbin, H. I., Joy, C. B., Cauble, A.E., Comeau, J. K., Patterson, J. M., and Needle, R. H. (1980). Family stress and coping: A decade review. *Journal of Marriage and the Family* 42(November): 125–141.

Mueller, E., and Ladd, W. (1970). Negro-white differences in geographic mobility. In C.V. Willie (Ed.) *The family life of black people.* Columbus OH: Charles E. Merrill, pp. 102–14.

Myers, H. (1982). Research on the Afro-American family: a critical review. In B. Bass, G. Wyatt, and G. Powell (Eds.) *The Afro-American family: Assessment, treatment, and research issues.* New York: Grune and Stratton, pp. 35–68.

Nobles, W. (1974) African root and American fruit: The black family. *Journal of Social and Behavioral Science* 20 (Spring): 66–77.

Nobles, W. (1976) *A formulative and empirical study of black families.* Contract no. 90-C-255. Washington: Office of Child Development.

Peters, M. F. (1974). The black family—Perpetuating the myths: An analysis of family sociology textbook treatment of black families. *Family Coordinator* 23(October): 349–57.

Peters, M. F. (1977). Nine black families: A study of household management and childrearing in black families with working mothers. Ed.D. diss. Harvard University, 1976. *Dissertation Abstracts International,* 37, p. 4648–A.

Peters, M. F. (1981). Parenting in black families with young children: A historical perspective. In H. P. McAdoo (Ed.) *Black families.* Beverly Hills: Sage Publications, pp. 211–24.

Peters, M. F., and Massey, G. (1983). Mundane extreme environmental stress in family stress theories: The case of black families in white America. *Marriage and Family Review* 6(Spring): 193–218.

Pierce, C. (1975) Mundane extreme environment and its effects on learning. In S. G. Brainard (Ed.) *Learning disabilities: Issues and recommendations for research*. Washington: National Institute of Education.

Pinderhughes, E. (1982). Afro-American families and the victim system. In M. McGoldrick, J. K. Pearce, and J. Giordano (Eds.) *Ethnicity and family therapy*. New York: Guilford Press, pp. 109–22.

Porter, J. R., and Washington, R. E. (1979). Black identity and self-esteem: A review of studies of black self-concept. *Annual Review of Sociology* 5: 53–74.

Rainwater, L. (1966), Crucible of identity: The Negro lower-class family. *Daedalus* 95(Winter): 172–216.

Reiss, D. (1981). *The family's construction of reality*. Cambridge, MA: Harvard University Press.

Reiss, D., and Oliveri, M. (1983). Family stress as community frame. *Marriage and Family Review* 6:61–83.

Roots III: Souls on Ice. *Newsweek*, June 10, 1985, pp. 82–84.

Rubin, L. B. (1976). *Worlds of pain*. New York: Basic Books.

Scanzoni, J. (1971) *The black family in modern society*. Boston: Allyn and Bacon.

Shimkin, D. B., and Louie, G. J., and Frate, D. A. (1978). The black extended family: A basic rural institution and a mechanism of urban adaptation. In D. B. Shimkin, E. M. Shimkin, and D. A. Frate (Eds.) (1978). *The extended family in black societies*. Chicago: Aldine, pp. 25–147.

Shimkin, D. B., Shimkin, E. M., and Frate, D. A. (Eds.)(1978). *The extended family in black societies*. Chicago: Aldine.

Simmons, R. (1978). Blacks and high self-esteem. *Social Psychology* 41(March): 54–57.

Slaughter, D. (1981). *Perspectives on the development of Afro-American children and their families: Part II* (Afro Scholar Working Papers). Urbana: University of Illinois Afro-American Studies and Research Program.

Spencer, M. B. (1982). Black children's racial values and parental patterns of child rearing. In G. McWorter (Ed.) *Studies on black children and their families*. Proceedings of the 6th Annual Conference of the National Council for Black Studies, March 17–20, 1982. Urbana: University of Illinois Afro-American Studies and Research Program, pp. D1–19.

Stack, C. (1974). *All our kin: Strategies for black survival in a black community.* New York: Harper and Row.

Sue, S., and Kitano, H. (1973). Stereotypes as a measure of success. *Journal of Social Issues* 29(Summer): 83–98.

Tinker, J. (1982). Intermarriage and assimilation in a plural society: Japanese-Americans in the United States. *Marriage and Family Review* 5(Summer): 61–74.

U.S. Bureau of the Census. (1978). *Social and economic status of the black population in the U.S.: A historical view 1790–1978.* Current Population Reports, Special Studies, P–32, #80.

Williams, L. For blacks, suburbs proving both pleasant and troubling. *The New York Times*, May 20, 1985 pp, A1, B4.

Willie, C. V. (1976). *A new look at black families.* Bayside, NY: General Hall.

Willie, C. V. (1981). *A new look at black families.* 2d ed. Bayside, NY: General Hall.

Willie, C.V., and Greenblatt, S. (1978) Four "classic" studies of power relationships in black families: A review and look to the future. *Journal of Marriage and the family* 40(November): 691–694.

Wilson, W. J. (1978). *The declining significance of race.* Chicago: University of Chicago Press.

Wyatt, G. E. (1982). Alternatives to the use of standardized tests with Afro-American children. In B. Bass, G. Wyatt, and G. Powell (eds.) *The Afro-American family: Assessment, treatment, and research issues.* New York: Grune and Stratton, pp. 119–36.

Young, V. H. (1970). Family and childhood in a southern Negro community. *American Anthropologist* 72(April): 269–88.

Young, V. H. (1974). A Black American socialization pattern. *American Ethnologist*, 1(August): 405–13.

Index

ABOUT THE AUTHOR

BEVERLY DANIEL TATUM, Ph.D. is an associate professor in the Department of Psychology and Education at Mount Holyoke College in South Hadley, Massachusetts. Dr. Tatum teaches courses on the psychology of racism as well as theories of personality and the psychology of the family. She has lectured extensively on the impact of social issues in the classroom. She is currently involved in research on racial identity development among Black youth in predominantly White settings. A graduate of Wesleyan University and the University of Michigan, Dr. Tatum is also a licensed clinical psychologist with a private practice in Northampton, Massachusetts.